Photograph by Studio Lautrec

Susan Vollmer grew up in New England, hundreds of miles from the nearest tortilla, tamale, or enchilada. She developed a love for Mexican food after living in Texas and discovering the local Mexican food there, with its delicious combinations of spicy ingredients.

Susan has studied with a number of cooking experts and has co-authored two cookbooks. She currently lives in Southern California with her husband, Chris, where she teaches cooking classes and gives cooking demonstrations.

◄═ Orange-Onion-Avocado Salad (page 129)

◄═ Black Bean Soup (page 38)

Spiced Meatloaf.

1/2 C. red chili sauce
2 tbsp. mustard powder
2 lbs. ground beef or pork
1 med. onion, chopped
1 egg, beaten
1 C. bread crumbs
Salt & pepper to taste
1 C. water
1/2 C tomato sauce
2 tbsp vinegar
2 tbsp brown sugar
2 tbsp. pineapple juice
Pineapple rings

Combine beef, onion, egg
bread crumbs, Salt & pepper &
chili sauce. Form into a loaf
& place in baking pan.
Make a sauce of the mustard,
water, tomato sauce, vinegar, sugar
& pineapple juice. Spread this sauce
over loaf & top with pineapple rings. Basting frequently
Bake at 350° for 1 1/2 hrs.   with the juices.

To Laura . . . for your cherished friendship
and constant support.

Authentic
MEXICAN
Cooking

by **Susan Vollmer**

Copyright 1987
Nitty Gritty Productions
P.O. Box 2008
Benicia, CA 94510-2008

A Nitty Gritty Cookbook
Printed by Mariposa Press
Benicia, California

ISBN 0-911954-84-8

Editor: Laura Wilson
Art Director: Mike Nelson
Photographer: Glen Millward
Food Stylist: Bobbie Greenlaw

Special thanks to Creative Cookware (Concord, CA)
and to Nordstrom's (Walnut Creek, CA) for the
cookware and props in our photographs.

Table of Contents

Introduction

Mexican cuisine evolved from the Aztec grandeur (corn was used in the ceremonial worship of the Aztec goddess of fertility) and the Mayan Indians with their diet of corn and beans. It reflects all the splendid cultures in its fascinating history. Because it is a food of the people, preparation is not regimented nor requires any frightening techniques. The foundation of Mexican cuisine is a diversity of thick sauces served over meats and vegetables.

Mexico has 6 regions - each with its own distinct flavors and traditions, textures and smells. The hot and dry North is known for cheese and flour tortillas. The Aztec culture influences Central Mexico as home of corn - corn tortillas and tamales. West-Central Mexico is truly mestizo and home of the mariachis and tequila. The hot and moist South has an abundance of tropical fruits and vegetables plus a remarkable variety of dried peppers. The Gulf States have well-stocked coastal waters for wonderful seafood and cool mountains for superb coffee. The Yucatan, half on the Gulf and half on Caribbean waters, is Mayan. Regional specialities include anchiote seasoning, pork wrapped in banana leaves and spicy black beans.

Unlike what we typically find here in the United States, Mexican food is not oily, heavy or necessarily highly seasoned. It is an extremely healthy diet with beans and corn for protein and carbohydrates, corn for calcium, and chilies for vitamins A and C. Besides, where else but in Mexico can you find such colorful, festive food.

Mexicans are dedicated to snacking - street eating is a national past time as evidenced by the abundance of street vendors. However, Mexicans still have their traditional comida (mid-day meal which can last 2-3 hours and consists of at least 5 courses). A typical meal can have a soup (often chicken broth based), rice (from tomato-red to herb-green), a fish course, and then the main course of meat or poultry in a delicious sauce (maybe served with potatoes and vegetables), then comes the ever-present beans, salad and finally dessert and coffee.

Even though none of us may take on the task of preparing a full comida, I do hope you enjoy the diversity of tastes, colors and flavors in this book.

Seasonings

Mexican cuisine, like that of other countries, has its own distinctive herbs, spices and special ingredients typical of its authentic dishes. All of these listed are quite common and should be readily available at supermarkets.

Almonds - Used in mole and other sauces.

Anchiote Seeds - A rusty-red seed with a musty flavor. Used for color and flavor.

Basil - An herb with a sweet flavor and a pungent undertone.

Chili Powder - A blend of spices using chilies as the main ingredient. The color depends upon the chilies used. To control your seasoning, it may be best to use the powder of dried chilies only.

Cilantro - Sometimes called Chinese parsley, this is the leaf of the coriander plant. Highly aromatic with a strong, fresh flavor.

Cinnamon - A pungent sweet spice from the dried bark of the cinnamon tree. Used extensively in Mexican cooking. Sold either in sticks or ground.

Coriander - The dried berry of the plant. Sold whole or ground. Tastes somewhat like a combination of lemon peel and sage.

Cumin - A predominant flavor in chili powder. Used in various sauces.

Masa Harina - The special corn flour used to make tortillas or tamales. Do not use corn meal as a substitute because the texture is too coarse.

Oregano - A strong flavored herb with a slightly bitter undertone.

Pepitas - Pumpkin seeds used as a base for sauces.

Sesame Seeds - Used a great deal as a topping for breads or in sauces. Almost always toasted to a golden brown before using.

Tomatillos - The small, green, tart tomatoes that are the basis for green sauces. Covered with a papery husk. To use, remove the husk, cover them with water in a saucepan and simmer about 10 minutes or until soft. Drain and blend them in a food processor, with skins and seeds, to a smooth consistency if you desire.

All About Chilies . . .

Or at least a little bit about chilies since the subject can be more than a bit confusing. Not only are there dozens and dozens of varieties - each with their own characteristics (flavor and degree of hotness) - but local names change from region to region. Also, many peppers are called one name when fresh and another one when dried. Since they are a basic element of Mexican cooking, here is some general information:

Fresh:

Anaheim (California green) - A fresh pepper, long and tapered, usually a bright green and mild in flavor. This chile is also found canned (2 or 3 whole to a 4-oz can).

Habanero - A light green chile shaped like a small lantern. It has the reputation of being the hottest chile. Used either fresh or roasted in sauces.

Poblano - A triangular shaped chile with an undulating surface. Used to make chiles rellenos.

Jalapeno - A very hot chile with a smooth surface. Available fresh, canned or pickled. Used in sauces.

Serrano - A small slender chile with a smooth surface. Used raw in sauces. Dynamite hot!

Dried:

Ancho - The most commonly used chile in Mexico. Tapered and dark-red but becomes brick-red when soaked. A good base for sauces. (Called chile negro in California).

Chile de Arbol - Long, skinny and brilliant red with a vicious bite.

Chile Japone - Similar to a Chile de Arbol but without a stem. This one breathes fire.

Chipotle - A dried, smoked jalapeno. Use to season stews and soups.

Pasilla - A long, slender, dark-brown chile. Used roasted and ground as a basis for sauces.

Pequin - A tiny, round pepper with an orangish-red skin. Extremely hot.

The chief misconception about chilies is their red-hot reputation. Many **are** hot, but others are sweet and mild. The incendiary culprit is an oil, capsaicin, in the vein or ribs near the seeds and in the seed pods - not in the seeds themselves. The seeds are hot only by association. You may want to wear thin rubber gloves when handling chilies since capsaicin can linger on your fingers for hours (causing them to burn).

Preparation - Dried Chilies:

Chilies are treated in different ways depending on usage and region:

- To soften, rinse in water. Then, cut open and discard the stems and seeds. Cut into small pieces and soak in water for about an hour.

- To toast, place on a griddle and turn from time to time until skin is charred and chilies crackle and blister. Then soak as above.

- Toast chilies, clean them, let them cool and grind them.

Preparation - Fresh Chilies:

If a recipe calls for roasted and peeled chilies, place them under the broiler, turning often until peppers are charred on all sides. (Or, spear with a fork and turn over high flame of a gas stove until charred.) Then, place in a plastic bag and close tightly. Let sit and steam for 10 minutes so skin peels away easily. Finally, skin, seed and stem the chilies. This would most often be done to Anaheim and Poblano chiles. Jalapeno and Serrano chiles are more often used raw (or maybe boiled) - seeded and chopped.

Appetizers

Whenever Mexicans are hungry, they have an endless array of foods to nibble on along the streets from a parade of street vendors. This gives us a tremendous wealth of delectable snacks to choose from when preparing Mexican appetizers. Actually, many foods served as main dishes by restaurants in the United States are mere appetizers to Mexicans, with tacos and tostados as excellent examples.

For lighter fare, appetizers are included that go well with a drink before dinner.

Guacamole

In Mexico, this is often eaten at the beginning of the meal with warm tortillas or with tacos and sour cream. It is used also as a sauce for meats and as a dressing for salads.

3 large avocados, peeled, seeded & mashed
2 tomatoes, diced
1/2 cup chopped onion
2 jalapeno or serrano peppers, minced
2 cloves garlic, minced
3 T. finely chopped Cilantro
juice of 1 lime
salt and pepper to taste

Mix all the ingredients together in a glass or plastic bowl. Cover surface directly with plastic wrap and refrigerate 30 minutes to blend flavors. Serve with tortilla chips.

Chile Con Queso

Yield: about 4 cups

A famous dish from Northern Mexico: You can ladle this directly over crisp tortillas or serve from a chafing dish as a dip.

1 T. vegetable oil
1 large onion, chopped
1 clove garlic, minced
1 T. flour
1 T. chili powder
1 (16 oz) can tomatoes, drained
1 (4 oz) can diced green chilies, drained
2 jalapeno peppers, chopped
1 lb. mild Cheddar cheese, shredded

In skillet saute garlic and onion in oil for about 5 minutes. Stir in flour and chili powder. Cook for 1 minute, stirring constantly. Add tomatoes, chilies and peppers and continue cooking until thickened, about 5 minutes. Over low heat, gradually add the cheese and stir until cheese is completely melted. Serve hot.

Guacamole (page 15)
Marinated Mushrooms (page 26) ➡

Quesadilla

These are like small, filled "turnovers." For variation, you may add a slice of ham or a spoonful of refried beans. For the chilies you may want to use the mild canned chilies or for more warmth, a jalapeno.

6 flour tortillas
1-1/2 cups shredded Monterey Jack or Cheddar cheese
6 T. diced green chilies
3 T. chopped green onion

Sprinkle the cheese over half of each tortilla. Top with some green chilies and green onion. Fold the tortillas in half. Place in a frying pan or on the grill to brown the tortillas and melt the cheese. Cut into quarters and serve hot.

◄▪ Squash Blossom Soup (page 32)

Chorizo

This mexican spicy sausage is used in many dishes. Here it is used to top a baked cheese appetizer.

1 T. chili powder
1 tsp. cumin
1/4 cup wine vinegar
3 T. tequila
2 garlic cloves, finely minced
1-1/2 tsp. oregano
1 tsp. paprika
1/2 tsp. salt
1/4 tsp. pepper
1/4 tsp. sugar
pinch of ground cloves
1/4 lb. ground beef
1/2 lb. ground pork

Mix all ingredients in glass or plastic bowl. Cover and refrigerate at least 24 hours to blend flavors. Keep no longer than 4 days. Cook in a skillet until thoroughly cooked.

Queso Asado

A traditional dish of baked cheese topped with spicy Mexican sausage.

6 cups of shredded cheese
    Use a combination of Cheddar, Muenster,
    Mozzarella and Jack
Chorizo (page 18)

   Place the cheese in a shallow baking dish. Top with the chorizo. Bake uncovered in a 350° oven until cheese is thoroughly melted - about 20 minutes.

Albondigas

Mexicans enjoy many variations of meatballs and commonly use them coated with a sauce as an appetizer or in soup.

Meatballs:
1-1/2 lb. ground beef
1 beaten egg
1 garlic clove, minced
1 mint leaf, minced
3 T. minced onion
1/3 cup bread crumbs
1 T. minced cilantro
1 T. minced green chilies
1 T. cumin
1 tsp. salt
1/2 tsp. thyme

Sauce:
1 cup red sauce (page 131)
1 cup beef broth

Combine all ingredients for meatballs in large mixing bowl. Shape into 1" balls. Heat the red sauce and beef broth in large saucepan. Add the meatballs and simmer until meat is cooked, about 30 minutes. Serve hot in a chafing dish.

Carnitas

Literally translated this means "little meats" and is a popular dish throughout central Mexico. Serve with salsa or guacamole and wrap in a warm tortilla.

2 lbs. pork shoulder, butt or country style spareribs
1 tsp. salt
1/4 tsp. pepper
2 cloves garlic, minced
1/4 tsp. cumin
juice of 2 oranges

Cut the pork into 1" cubes, leaving some fat on the pieces. Place in a dutch oven and barely cover with water. Add the salt, pepper, garlic and cumin. Simmer until the water is almost evaporated. Add the orange juice and continue cooking about an hour or until the meat is lightly browned.

Tacos

A tortilla wrapped around just about anything. Mexicans are most apt to use soft tortillas, but here is a recipe for crisp-fried tortillas.

8 tortillas, corn or flour
1/2 cup vegetable oil

Garnishes:
1 cup shredded lettuce
1 tomato, cut into strips
1 avocado, cut into slivers
1 cup chopped red onion
1 cup shredded Cheddar cheese
1 cup sour cream
1 cup green sauce (page 134)

In a skillet, heat the oil. One by one, place a tortilla in the oil. After a few seconds, fold the tortilla in half and fry until crisp. Drain on paper towels. Insert the filling and top with a choice of garnishes.

Fillings:

Chicken:
2 T. butter
2 cups shredded cooked chicken
1 T. chili powder
1/2 tsp. cumin

1 (4 oz) can diced green chilies
2 green onions, chopped
1 tomato, skinned and chopped
salt and pepper, to taste

Melt the butter in a skillet and add the remaining ingredients. Cook until heated through.

Beef:
1 T. vegetable oil
1/2 onion, chopped
1 clove garlic, minced
2 cups shredded cooked beef

3 tomatoes, skinned and chopped
1 T. chili powder
1/2 tsp. cumin

Heat the oil and saute the onion and garlic 5 minutes. Add the meat and brown. Add the remaining ingredients and cook another 5 mintues to heat through.

Ceviche

This is an extremely popular appetizer in Mexico. The raw fish or shellfish is marinated in lemon and lime juices until it has the appearance and taste of having been poached.

1-1/2 lbs. fresh scallops or mild-flavored
   fish such as sole or halibut
juice of 3 limes
juice of 3 lemons
1 medium red onion, chopped
1/4 cup chopped cilantro
1 sweet red pepper, finely chopped

1 green pepper, finely chopped
2 tomatoes, peeled, seeded and diced
3 scallions, chopped
1/4 cup olive oil
1 tsp. oregano
salt and pepper, to taste
3 chiles serranos (optional)

Cut the fish into small pieces. Place it in a glass bowl along with the lime and lemon juice. Refrigerate at least 6 hours or until the fish becomes opaque. Add the remaining ingredients and refrigerate at least another hour to blend the flavors.

Serve with tortilla chips.

Chile Nuts

These spicy nuts make a wonderful addition to icy cold beer or frosty Margaritas.

2 cups salted, skinless peanuts
2 T. ground red chili powder
1 tsp. onion powder
1/2 tsp. garlic powder
olive oil

Place the nuts in a large baking pan with sides. Mix the spices together in a bowl and sprinkle over the nuts. Drizzle with a little bit of olive oil if the spices do not stick to the nuts.

Heat in a 250° oven for 15 minutes. Using a spatula, turn the nuts over and cook for another 5 minutes.

Serve warm.

Marinated Mushrooms

A fresh, tangy citrus marinade accented with cilantro.

1/2 cup water
3 T. vegetable oil
1/4 cup fresh orange juice
1/4 cup fresh lemon juice
2 strips lemon peel
2 strips orange peel
1 T. sugar
1-1/2 tsp. salt
1-1/2 tsp. mustard seed
1/2 tsp. oregano
2 T. chopped cilantro
1/2 tsp. freshly ground pepper
1 lb. mushrooms, medium size, stems removed

Combine all the ingredients in a large saucepan. Bring to a simmer and remove from the heat. Place in a glass bowl and marinate in the refrigerator for at least 24 hours.

Serve at room temperature.

Tortas

This is Central Mexico's version of a submarine sandwich. Although more a snack than an appetizer, cut the roll into individual servings for smaller appetites.

4 crusty Italian rolls
2 cups warm refried beans
3 chicken breasts, cooked and shredded
4 slices Cheddar cheese
1 tomato, sliced
1 avocado, peeled & sliced
shredded lettuce

Garnish: strips of canned green chilies,
jalapenos or red cherry peppers

Cut each roll in half and remove some of the soft center. Spread the bottom half with beans. Then, layer the remaining ingredients and top with the other roll half. Garnish with peppers.
Variation: Use slices of ham or cooked pork instead of or together with the chicken.

Soups

Wherever you go in Mexico, regardless of how hot and humid the climate is, soup will appear as a prelude to a traditional Mexican meal. Soups run the gamut from a clear broth or light cream soup to a thick combination of meats and beans. Cooks of each region have developed their own specialities to make use of the fresh local ingredients.

The soups in this chapter are ''wet'' and served as the meal's first course. The Mexican sopa seca (or ''dry'' soup) is basically rice, hominy, pasta or other heavy grained dishes served as a course after the wet soup.

Cheese Soup

A simple peasant soup from Sonora in Northern Mexico. This is a light version with a base of chicken broth and tomatoes with shredded cheese added at the end.

2 T. butter
1 large onion, chopped
3 cloves garlic, minced
6 cups chicken broth
4 medium tomatoes, peeled & diced

1 large canned, peeled chile
1/4 cup chopped cilantro
salt & pepper, to taste
2 cups shredded Monterey Jack cheese
2 cups shredded mild Cheddar cheese

In stockpot, melt butter and saute onion and garlic about 5 minutes. Stir in broth, tomatoes, chile and cilantro. Bring to a boil, reduce heat, cover and simmer for 10 minutes. Season with salt and pepper.

Just before serving, stir in the cheese. Serve the soup as soon as the cheese is melted.

Tortilla Soup

The most characteristic soup of Mexico and one of the most popular. Its base is chicken broth with crisp strips of tortillas and lots of dried chile. Lime brings out the flavor.

2 T. vegetable oil
1 medium onion, chopped
2 cloves garlic, minced
2 tomatoes, peeled
6 cups chicken broth
salt, to taste
1 tsp. chili powder
1/2 tsp. cumin
1/3 cup vegetable oil
6 corn tortillas, cut into 1/2" strips
2 dried chile pasilla, stemmed & seeded
2 cups shredded Monterey Jack cheese
1-2 limes, cut into wedges

In large saucepan saute onion and garlic in oil until golden brown. Put in blender with tomatoes and process until smooth. Pour into large saucepan and cook about 5 minutes or until thick. Stir in broth and simmer 20 minutes. Season with salt, chili powder and cumin.

In skillet, fry tortilla strips in oil until crisp. Drain. Add to soup and cook another 5 minutes. Cut chilies into small pieces and fry in same oil about 5 seconds. Remove and drain.

To serve, divide cheese among 6 soup bowls, ladle the hot soup on top and sprinkle chilies on top. Pass the lime.

Squash Blossom Soup

One of the most delicious soups I know anywhere. If you don't have a vegetable garden, or can't find squash blossoms, chopped summer or crookneck squash can be used.

4 T. butter
1 small onion, chopped
2 cloves garlic, minced
1/2 cup fresh mushrooms, sliced
1/2 lb. (20 large) squash blossoms, chopped
1 cup fresh corn kernels
6 cups chicken broth
salt and pepper, to taste
2 T. chopped cilantro
1/2 cup Monterey Jack or Mozzarella cheese, cubed

Melt the butter in a skillet and saute the onion, garlic, mushrooms, and squash blossoms for 5 minutes. Meanwhile, in a large saucepan, combine the corn, broth, salt and pepper and cilantro. Simmer about 10 minutes. Stir in the sauteed vegetables and simmer another 5 minutes. Add the cheese cubes and serve.

Eggs Yucatan Style (page 56) ⟼

Corn and Green Vegetable Soup

Serves 6

Since corn is **the** staple of Mexico, I have to include a corn soup recipe. This one is very delicious and a bit unusual.

1/2 stick unsalted butter
1/2 onion, chopped
2 cloves garlic, minced
2/3 cup tomatillos, cooked
4-1/2 cups corn kernels
5 cups chicken broth
2/3 cup green peas

2 T. chopped cilantro
2 chiles poblano, roasted & peeled
3 large lettuce leaves
1 tsp. salt
Garnish:
1/2 cup sour cream
tortilla strips, crisp-fried

Melt the butter in a large saucepan and saute the onion and garlic about 5 minutes. In a blender, puree the tomatillos until smooth. Add to the saucepan. Cook over high heat about 4 minutes.

In a bowl, combine the corn, 2 cups of the chicken broth, peas, cilantro, chilies and lettuce. Bit by bit, puree in blender until smooth and add to the pan. Cook about 5 minutes. Then, add the remaining broth and salt. Simmer the soup until slightly thickened, about 20 minutes.

When serving, garnish with sour cream and tortilla strips.

◀▦ Chiles Relenos de Queso (page 112)

Chicken Lime Soup

Serves 8

This is **the** soup of the Yucatan. Even on the hottest day, you will be served a steaming bowl of lime soup. The soup gets its distinctive taste from the limes grown only on the Yucatan Peninsula, but we can duplicate the authentic flavor by combining our limes with a bit of grapefruit peel.

8 cups chicken broth
3 chicken breasts
4 chicken livers (optional)
1/2 cup chopped onion
1 clove garlic, minced
2 T. vegetable oil
2 large tomatoes, skinned and diced
1/2 cup chopped green pepper
1/2 tsp. oregano
4 slices grapefruit peel
3 T. fresh lime juice

Garnish:
6 corn tortillas, cut into strips & crisp fried
lime slices
1/3 cup diced serrano chile

In a stock pot, combine the chicken broth and chicken breasts. Simmer 15 minutes. Add the livers and simmer 10 minutes more. Remove and finely chop the livers and shred the breasts. Strain broth, and return to stock pot.

In skillet, saute the onion and garlic in oil about 5 minutes. Add the tomatoes, green pepper and oregano. Cook another 5 minutes and stir into broth. Add the grapefruit peel and lime juice. Simmer 20 minutes and add the chicken. Heat thoroughly and remove peel.

When ready to serve, divide the tortilla strips among the soup bowls. Ladle the soup over and garnish with lime slices and diced chile.

Albondigas Soup

Moist meatballs poached in a stock along with a medley of fresh vegetables.

Stock:
6 cups chicken broth
1 T. minced mint leaves
1 tsp. salt
1/2 tsp. pepper
3 cloves garlic, minced

1 albondigas recipe (page 20)

1 T. butter
2 green bell peppers, sliced
1 cup sliced onion
1 cup chopped carrot
1/2 cup chopped celery
1 cup diced tomatoes
1 (4 oz) can chopped green chilies

Put stock ingredients into a large stockpot. Add the meatballs and bring to a boil over high heat. Reduce heat and simmer, skimming fat from the surface, for about 15 minutes.

Meanwhile, melt the butter in a large frying pan. Add all the vegetables except tomatoes and chilies. Saute about 10 minutes. Add to the soup along with the tomatoes and chilies. Stir thoroughly. Simmer about 10 minutes.

Creamy Cold Avocado Soup

This can also be served hot by warming the soup as the final step.

3 large ripe avocados, peeled
salt and pepper
1 tsp. ground mild red chile
1/8 tsp. nutmeg
1 cup cold heavy cream
6 cups chicken broth
1/2 cup dry sherry

Puree the avocados in a food processor until smooth. Season with salt and pepper. Add chile and nutmeg. Beat in the cream. Remove to a bowl.

In a saucepan over medium heat cook chicken broth and sherry for 5 minutes. Set aside and let cool. Then, blend into avocado mixture. Refrigerate for at least 4 hours to allow flavors to blend.

Black Bean Soup

Black (or black turtle beans) are small, mild-flavored beans used in both Mexican and South American cuisines. If you prefer a smooth-texture, puree the soup before serving.

1 lb. dry black beans, soaked in water overnight
1/4 cup vegetable oil
1 large onion, diced
4 cloves garlic, minced
1 smoked ham hock
3 qts. water
1 T. cumin
1 tsp. oregano
1 bay leaf
1 tsp. freshly ground pepper
1/8 tsp. cayenne pepper
1 tsp. salt
1/4 cup chopped cilantro
3 T. dry sherry
1 T. lemon juice
1 cup sour cream

Garnish:
diced avocado
chopped onion

In stockpot, heat the vegetable oil and saute onion and garlic about 5 minutes. Drain the beans and add them to pot along with the hamhock, water, cumin, oregano, bay leaf, pepper and cayenne pepper. Bring to a boil and reduce heat. Cook, uncovered, until beans are tender, about 1-1/2 - 2 hours. Stir in the salt.

Remove ham hock. Pull off any remaining meat, shred and return meat to pot. Stir in the cilantro, sherry and lemon juice. Simmer another 30 minutes. When serving, spoon the sour cream on top of each bowl. Garnish with avocado and onion.

Gazpacho

From Mexico's Spanish heritage comes this cool, smooth soup studded with diced vegetables.

6 large tomatoes, skinned & seeded
1/3 cup olive oil
2 T. wine vinegar
2 cloves garlic
1 tsp. cumin
4 slices white bread, cubed
1-1/2 cups water
salt and pepper, to taste

Garnish:
1 cucumber, diced
1 green pepper, diced
3 green onions, diced

Place all the ingredients in a blender. Blend until smooth. Refrigerate until cold, at least an hour.

When serving, pass the garnishes around in separate bowls.

Chilled Tomatillo Soup

A refreshing and unusual way to start a meal on a hot summer night.

2 T. vegetable oil
2 jalapeno chilies, diced
1 small onion, chopped
2 lbs. tomatillos, husked and quartered
4 cups chicken broth
salt, to taste
2 T. chopped cilantro

Heat the oil in a large saucepan, and add the chilies and onion. Cook about 10 minutes. Add the tomatillos and broth. Bring to a boil, reduce heat, cover and simmer until tomatillos are tender, about 15 minutes. Season with salt. Transfer soup to a blender and puree until smooth. Chill completely.

When serving, garnish with cilantro.

Tortillas, Tamales and Eggs

When ancient Mexicans invented tortillas, they invented the most versatile bread of all. Tortillas are an indispensable part of every Mexican meal. They are stacked, rolled, folded, softened, crisp-fried or toasted. The first ones were made of native corn, with dried kernals simmered in water with lime until soft, then ground by hand. Flour tortillas are a speciality of the wheat-growing area of Northern Mexico. This tortilla recipe, however, is for the more commonly used corn tortillas.

To make a tamale, wrap dried corn husks around a coating of masa dough to seal in the tasty filling. Tamales are fiesta food, a Sunday special in restaurants and the ceremonial dish made on All Saint's Day.

Eggs are prepared a variety of ways in Mexico and always accompanied by warm tortillas and refried beans.

How To Make Tortillas

Four tortillas can be made from regular all purpose flour, but corn tortillas require the special corn preparation called masa harina which is widely distributed by The Quaker Oats Company.

Tortillas can be patted into shape by hand, but this requires practise. You can easily roll dough out with a rolling pin. But for the quickest and best results, you may want to buy an inexpensive tortilla press.

Corn Tortillas:
2 cups masa harina
1-1/4 cups warm water

In a bowl mix the dough together and shape into a smooth ball. Divide into 12 equal pieces and roll each into a ball. Makes 12 - 6″ tortillas.

Rolling pin method: Flatten a small ball of dough between 2 damp cloths. Roll with light even strokes. Remove cloths and trim tortilla to a round shape. Place between waxed paper and continue with remaining dough.

Tortilla Press: Place waxed paper on bottom half of press. Place a ball of dough on paper - slightly off center toward hinge of press. Flatten slightly with the palm of your hand. Cover with piece of waxed paper. Close the press and push handle down firmly.

To Cook: Remove top piece of waxed paper. Place tortilla down on preheated, ungreased griddle. As tortilla becomes warm, you will be able to peel off remaining paper.

Cook about 2 minutes, turning frequently, until tortilla is soft, but dry and lightly flecked with brown specs.

Serve immediately or let cool and wrap in an airtight package. Refrigerate or freeze. To serve, reheat by placing on preheated griddle about 30 seconds each side or wrap in foil and place in 350° oven about 15 minutes. To keep hot for several hours, wrap in foil and then in a cloth or 12 to 14 sheets of newspaper. Tortillas will stay hot for about 2 hours in the paper wrapping.

Flour Tortillas:
3 cups all purpose flour
2 tsp. baking powder
3/4 tsp. salt
2 T. lard
1 cup warm water

In a bowl combine dry ingredients. Cut in lard until particles are fine. Add water gradually. Form into a ball and knead about 5 minutes. Cover with towel and let rest 20 minutes. Use rolling pin method to roll out the tortillas. Makes 10 - 7″ tortillas.

Enchiladas Suizas

A spicy chicken and cheese filling topped with a soothing sour cream sauce.

2 T. vegetable oil
1 medium onion, diced
1 clove garlic, minced
1/2 cup sliced green olives
1 (4 oz) can green chilies
1 T. chili powder
1/4 cup chopped cilantro
1 tsp. cumin
salt and pepper, to taste
3 cups shredded cooked chicken

12 tortillas
vegetable oil
1 cup water
1/4 cup taco sauce

3 cups shredded Jack cheese

Sauce:
1/2 cup butter
1/4 cup flour
2 cups milk
2 cups sour cream

Heat oil in skillet and saute onion and garlic 5 minutes. Stir in green olives, chilies, chili powder, cilantro and cumin. Season with salt and pepper. Add chicken and cook until heated through.

Fry the tortillas quickly in the oil. Remove and drain on paper towels. Combine the water and taco sauce in a bowl and dip each tortilla into the mixture.

Spread chicken mixture down the center of each tortilla. Sprinkle 2 tablespoons of cheese over chicken and roll up. Place in baking dish.

Sauce: Melt butter in saucepan. Whisk in flour. Blend in milk. Heat to a boil and simmer until thickened. Stir in sour cream. Pour sauce over enchiladas and sprinkle with additional shredded cheese. Bake in a 375° oven about 25 minutes.

Acapulco Chicken Enchiladas

Slivered almonds give a pleasant crunchiness to the chicken filling.

12 tortillas
vegetable oil

Filling:
2 T. butter
3 cups diced cooked chicken or turkey
3/4 cup chopped ripe olives
1 cup slivered almonds
1/2 cup shredded mild Cheddar cheese
1/2 cup sauce

Sauce:
1 medium onion, minced
2 cloves garlic, minced
2 T. vegetable oil
3-1/2 cups tomato puree
4 T. chili powder
1/2 tsp. cumin
1/2 tsp. oregano
1 tsp. salt

Garnish:
1-1/2 cups shredded mild Cheddar cheese
2 cups sour cream

Filling: Melt the butter in a skillet and add the ingredients. Cook until heated through.

Sauce: Heat oil in a saucepan and cook onion and garlic 5 minutes. Add remaining ingredients and simmer 30 minutes. Pour through strainer.

To Assemble: Fry the tortillas quickly in oil, drain and dip in sauce. Place filling on each and roll tightly. Place side by side in baking dish. Spoon remaining sauce over and sprinkle with cheese. Bake in 350° oven 15 minutes. Top with sour cream.

Enchiladas with Chilies and Cheese

A classic enchilada - melted cheese and chilies inside - baked in a tomato and chile sauce. Your choice of ground red chile will dictate the heat.

12 tortillas
vegetable oil
3 cups red chile sauce
3 cups shredded Jack cheese
1 onion, chopped
1 (7 oz) can green chilies
2 cups sour cream

Quickly fry the tortillas in the oil. Drain on paper towels. Dip each into the sauce. Using 2 cups of the cheese, sprinkle some down the center of each, top with chopped onion and chilies cut into strips. Roll up and place in baking dish. Spoon sauce over top and sprinkle with remaining cheese. Bake at 350° for 15 minutes. Top with sour cream.

Red Chile Sauce:
2 tomatoes, peeled and seeded
2 T. vegetable oil
2 T. flour
1/4 to 1/2 cup ground red chile
2 cups beef broth
3/4 tsp. salt
1 clove garlic, minced
1/2 tsp. oregano
1/2 tsp. cumin

In a blender puree the tomatoes and set aside. Heat oil in a saucepan and whisk in flour. Stir until slightly browned. Add the ground chile into the broth (start with smaller amount and add more to taste). Gradually stir into flour and continue to stir until smooth. Add tomato puree, salt, garlic, oregano and cumin. Simmer for at least 10 minutes.

Burritos

Serves 4

This is similar to enchiladas only made with flour instead of corn tortillas.

8 flour tortillas
4 cups warm refried beans (page 120)
1 cup shredded lettuce
2 cups shredded Jack cheese
1 large tomato, sliced
1 avocado, sliced
8 green onions, chopped
2 cups green sauce (page 134)

Heat tortillas on a hot griddle, 30 seconds per side.

Spread the beans down the center of each tortilla. Top with remaining ingredients. Fold tortilla over the filling to completely enclose it. Place in a oven-proof dish and bake in a 350° oven for 20 minutes.

How To Make Tamales

The tamale making procedure is briefly this: Spread a corn husk with masa dough, put several spoonfuls of filling in center, then fold husk around filling to make a little packet. Place packets in a steamer and steam until masa dough is cooked and firm.

Dried corn husks are available at many grocery stores. Or dry your own by leaving green husks in a warm, sunny spot for 4-8 days or until yellow. However, fresh corn husks can be used. If all else fails, use pieces of tin foil or parchment paper. To prepare the dried husks - soak in warm water at least 2 hours.

Lay a husk flat. Spread 2 tablespoons masa dough in rectangle in center of husk. Keep margins around edge of dough. Spoon 2 tablespoons filling on center of dough and fold sides of husk over to center and then fold in the top and bottom of husk. Lay, folded side down. Tie with string if necessary.

Stack the tamales upright on a rack in large pan. Pour in hot water to just under rack level. Cover and simmer at least 1 hour. Tamales are done when the masa dough is firm and doesn't stick to the corn husk.

continued

How To Make Tamales continued

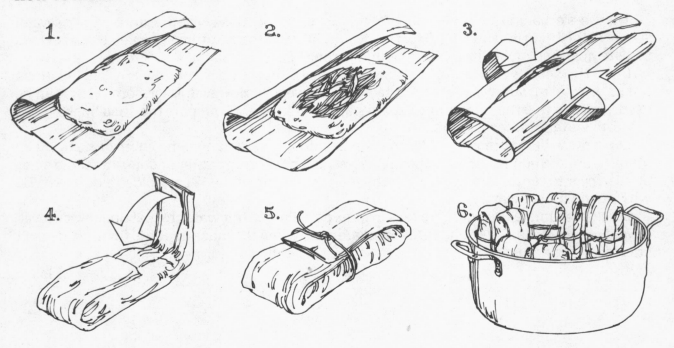

Tamales

Use the directions on the previous page for assembling these tamales.

Masa Dough:
1-1/3 cups lard, butter, or solid shortening
4 cups masa harina
2 tsp. salt
2-2/3 cups warm water or beef broth

Whip lard in a bowl until fluffy. Blend in remaining ingredients until dough holds together.

Filling: Fills 12 tamales
2 medium tomatoes, peeled
1 clove garlic, minced
1/4 tsp. salt
1/2 tsp. cumin

2 T. vegetable oil
1/4 onion, sliced
2 jalapeno chilies, diced
1-1/3 cups shredded cooked pork or beef

Blend the tomatoes, garlic, salt and cumin in a bowl until smooth. Heat the oil in a saucepan and saute the onion about 5 minutes. Add the jalapenos and tomato puree. Cook another 5 minutes. Add the pork and continue cooking about 10 minutes until fairly dry.

Eggs Yucatan Style

Serves 6

Huevos Rancheros with Yucatan flourishes.

12 tortillas
vegetable oil
12 eggs
1-1/2 cups warm refried beans
1 cup diced ham
1 cup cooked peas
1 cup shredded Jack cheese

Sauce:
1 small onion, chopped
3 garlic cloves, minced
2 T. vegetable oil

4 tomatoes, peeled & chopped
1-1/2 cups tomato sauce
1/2 cup diced green chilies
1/2 cup chicken broth

Garnish:
3 bananas, peeled
1/4 cup butter

    Cut the bananas in half lengthwise and saute in butter in a skillet until lightly browned. Fry the tortillas in vegetable oil until crisp. Remove and drain on paper towels. Fry the eggs. Spread the tortillas with beans and top with the eggs, ham and peas. Pour sauce over and sprinkle with cheese. Garnish with bananas.

    Sauce: Pour oil in a saucepan and saute onion and garlic 5 minutes. Stir in remaining ingredients and simmer 10 minutes.

Eggs with Avocado Sauce

Hard-cooked eggs under a smooth avocado sauce. Serve with fried ham or chorizo.

2 T. butter
2 T. onion, minced
1 Anaheim chile, roasted and peeled
1 T. flour
1/2 cup milk

8 eggs
2 avocados, peeled and diced
2 T. chopped cilantro
salt, to taste

Melt butter in a saucepan and saute the onion until tender. Seed and mince the chile. Add to the onion along with the flour. Cook a minute and gradually whisk in the milk. Cook, stirring constantly until thick.

Hard boil the eggs while you finish the sauce.

Puree the avocados in a blender and stir into the sauce along with the cilantro. Season with salt.

Peel the eggs and cut in half. Pour the sauce over top.

Scrambled Eggs with Chorizo

Serves 4

Piping hot corn or flour tortillas with butter make the perfect accompaniment.

8 oz. (1 cup) chorizo - store bought or homemade (page 18)
1 T. vegetable oil
1 onion, chopped
1 tomato, chopped
1 chile poblano, roasted & peeled, seeded & sliced
8 eggs
salt, to taste

Heat oil in a skillet and cook the chorizo, stirring to break up the clumps, about 10 minutes. Remove and discard all but 2 tablespoons fat from skillet. Add the onion, tomato and chile. Cook about 7 minutes or until onion is soft. Return chorizo to pan.

Quickly beat the eggs, add to the skillet and scramble until done to your liking. Season with salt.

Meats

Originally, Mexicans had to rely upon beans and corn for their protein before the Spaniards brought their cattle to the country in the 1500's.

Now, large steaks are cooked over wood fires in large, open air restaurants in Northern Mexico. Succulent cabrito is abundent in the northeast and central highlands. The milkfed kid, with its delicate, tender meat is slow roasted over embers. In Yucatan and Sonora, deer is a popular meat, deliciously mild and pit roasted. In Central and Southern Mexico, lamb is chile-marinated, roasted and steamed in avocado or banana leaves.

Mexico is a nation of pork lovers, with their pork described as legendary. The variations are numerous and bear witness to the great creativity of Mexican cooks.

Chile con Carne

Or, otherwise known in Texas as a "bowl of red." Although Texas "claims" to have invented "chile," it was around when the Spaniards met the American Indians.

2 T. vegetable oil
1 large onion, chopped
3 lbs. lean, tender beef, cubed
3 cloves garlic, minced
1/4 cup chili powder
1 T. cumin
1 tsp. oregano
2 tsp. salt
1/2 tsp. cayenne pepper
1 T. paprika
5 cups water

Heat oil in a dutch oven and saute the onion until soft. Add the meat, garlic, chili powder and cumin. Cook until the meat is browned. Add remaining ingredients and stir well. Simmer about 2 hours.

Beef Tips in Tomato-Chile Sauce

Tender cubes of beef simmered in a sauce to give it a special zest.

1-1/2 lbs. tender, boneless beef, cubed
2 T. vegetable oil
1 onion, sliced
3 chiles poblano, roasted,
    peeled, seeded & diced
2/3 cup beef broth
Tomato-Chile sauce

Tomato-Chile Sauce:
3 tomatoes (1-1/2 lbs), peeled & diced
4 chiles serranos, diced
1/2 onion, chopped
2 cloves garlic, minced
1 T. vegetable oil
salt

Heat oil in skillet, add beef, brown and cook to about medium-rare. Remove from skillet and add the onion, chilies, broth and tomato-chile sauce. Simmer 10 minutes. Return meat to skillet, heat and serve.

Sauce: Place the tomatoes, chilies, onion and garlic in a blender. Process until almost pureed. Heat the oil in a skillet and add the sauce. Cook about 5 minutes until slightly thickened. Season with salt.

Fajitas

Marinated steak, grilled, sliced and quickly fried with onions and green peppers. If you can't find skirt steak substitute flank steak. Serve with warm tortillas and Pico di Gallo (page 123).

1 cup fresh orange juice
1/2 cup vegetable oil
1/4 cup red wine vinegar
1 tsp. salt
1/2 tsp. freshly ground pepper
1 tsp. chili powder

1/2 tsp. cumin
2 garlic cloves, minced
2 lbs. skirt steak
2 large onions, sliced
2 large green peppers, sliced

Whisk together all the ingredients except steak, onions and peppers in a bowl. Place in a glass baking dish. Add the steak, cover and refrigerate overnight.

Remove from marinade. Grill or broil until crisp on the outside, but still pink inside. Thinly slice the steak. Fry it in a skillet with the onions and peppers until slightly charred and very hot.

Carne Tampiquena

These steaks take on a special flavor and tenderness from the vegetable stuffing and the wrapping of bacon.

6 New York strip steaks
18 slices bacon
2 T. butter
2 cups tomatoes, diced
3 Anaheim chiles, roasted, peeled
    & chopped
1 onion, chopped

2 cloves garlic, minced
1/4 lb. boiled ham, diced
1/4 cup chopped cilantro
salt & pepper, to taste
1/2 tsp. cumin
1 tsp. oregano
1 cup tomato sauce

Melt butter in a skillet and saute the tomatoes, chilies, onion, garlic and ham about 10 minutes. Add the spices and tomato sauce. Simmer 15 minutes.

Cut a pocket in each steak and fill with half the vegetable mixture. Wrap each steak with 3 slices of bacon.

Broil or grill the steaks. Reheat the remaining vegetable sauce and spoon over the steaks when serving.

Paella (page 92) ➡

Picadillo

Beef with a wonderful, unusually sweet, spicy flavor.

1 lb. lean beef, coarsely chopped
2 T. vegetable oil
1 onion, chopped
2 large tomatoes, diced
2 cloves garlic, minced
1/4 cup beef broth
2 T. apple cider vinegar
1 tsp. sugar
1 tsp. ground cinnamon
1/8 tsp. ground cloves
1/2 tsp. cumin
1 tsp. salt
1/2 cup seedless raisins
1/2 cup slivered almonds

Heat oil in a large skillet and brown the meat. Add the onion and cook 5 minutes. Add the remaining ingredients except the almonds. Simmer about 45 minutes. Add the almonds just before serving.

◀▥ Red Snapper Veracruz (page 87)

Pork Chops Adobo

Pork chops marinated in a paste made of chilies, herbs, spices and vinegar. Serve with a red salsa and sour cream.

4 chiles anchos, toasted and seeded
1/4 tsp. cumin
1/4 tsp. oregano
1/4 tsp. thyme
1 T. salt

2 cloves garlic
1/2 cup white vinegar
6 pork chops
2 T. vegetable oil

Soak the chilies for 20 minutes in hot water. Transfer to a blender and add all the other ingredients except the pork and oil. Puree to a smooth paste. Spread on both sides of the pork chops. Refrigerate overnight.

Fry the chops **very slowly** in the oil until done - about 30 minutes. Then raise the heat and brown the pork very quickly.

Pork in Green Sauce

Serves 6

A boneless pork loin braised in a tart sauce of tomatillos which add a piquancy to this dish.

3 lbs. boneless pork loin
1 onion, sliced
1/2 tsp. oregano
2 cloves garlic
1 tsp. salt
1 tsp. black pepper

Sauce:
1 clove garlic
1 onion
1 cup tomatillos, cooked
1/4 cup cilantro
1/3 cup green chilies
2 T. vegetable oil
1 cup water
1 tsp. oregano
salt and pepper, to taste

Place the pork and remaining ingredients in a stockpot. Add water to barely cover the meat. Cover and simmer 2 hours. Meanwhile, start sauce.

Puree the garlic, onion, tomatillos, cilantro and chilies in a blender. Heat oil in a large sauce-pan and saute this mixture for 5 minutes. Stir in the water. Add the oregano, salt and pepper.

When meat is done, slice and add it to the sauce. Simmer 20 mintues. Arrange pork on platter and spoon sauce over.

Roast Pork with Pumpkin Seed Sauce

Serves 4

Originally it was the Mayans who cultivated pumpkins and used the seeds in their food. These sauces are among the earliest recorded preparations of food.

1 ancho chile
1/4 cup sugar
2 T. coarse salt
1 tsp. rosemary
1 tsp. pepper
2 to 2-1/2 lbs. boneless pork loin
1 T. olive oil

Sauce:
2 poblano chiles
1 cup shelled raw pumpkin seeds (pepitas)
2-1/2 cups chicken broth
2 toasted white bread slices
1/2 cup cilantro, chopped
1/2 onion, chopped
2 cloves garlic, minced
2 T. butter
1 cup heavy cream

Stem, seed and mince the ancho chile. Place in a bowl, add next 4 ingredients and mix well. Rub over the pork, cover and refrigerate overnight.

Heat olive oil in a skillet and brown the pork. Roast in a 350° oven about 1 hour or until done. Cut pork into slices. Arrange on a platter and spoon the sauce over.

Sauce: Roast, peel and seed the chilies. Heat a skillet, add the pumpkin seeds and toast until they pop. Put into blender with the chilies, broth, toast, cilantro, onion and garlic. Puree until smooth. Melt the butter in a saucepan. Stir in the puree and simmer 15 minutes. Add the cream and bring to a boil.

Guiso de Puerco

An exotic name for the most delicious pork stew you will ever taste.

2 lbs. boneless pork, cubed
1/4 cup flour
1/2 cup vegetable oil
1 onion, chopped
2 slices bacon, diced
1/2 cup water
4 fresh tomatoes, chopped
3 potatoes, diced

2 T. orange juice
2 T. lime juice
1/4 cup tequila
2 tsp. cumin
1 tsp. oregano
1 tsp. thyme
salt and pepper
1/2 cup sour cream

Coat the pork with flour. Heat oil in large skillet and saute the pork until brown. Remove and set aside. Add the onion and bacon to the skillet and cook until bacon is crisp. Stir in the pork and remaining ingredients except sour cream. Cover and simmer until pork is tender, about 45 minutes. Remove from the heat and stir in the sour cream.

Chile Verde

The mild Anaheim chilies season this pork stew. Serve it with rice or as a filling for burritos (wrap in flour tortillas and serve with sour cream and diced tomato).

1 lb. Anaheim chiles
1-1/2 lbs. lean pork, cubed
2 T. vegetable oil
2 jalapeno chiles, minced
2 onions, chopped
3 tomatoes, chopped
1/4 cup chopped cilantro

2 cloves garlic, minced
2 tomatoes, pureed
1 cup water
2 tsp. salt
1/2 tsp. freshly ground black pepper
1 tsp. oregano

Roast, peel and chop the Anaheim chiles. Heat oil in large skillet and saute the pork until brown. Add the Anaheims, jalapenos, onions, chopped tomatoes, cilantro and garlic. Simmer 15 minutes. Add the pureed tomatoes, water and seasonings. Simmer for about 1 hour, stirring occasionally.

Chicken

Chicken was brought into Mexico by the Spaniards and soon became the most popular meat in Mexico, as well as the best selling fowl in the markets. Wild turkey, however, is the original Mexican fowl and is still commonly raised throughout Mexico. It is also the traditional bird for the festive Mole Poblano.

You won't find the juicy, plump chickens that we're accustomed to in the United States. Most Mexican chicken is too tough for dry roasting or frying and is generally simmered, steamed or braised in an array of sauces until tender.

Pollo con Rajas

A creamy casserole of chicken breasts and strips of chilies. It has a very slight picante flavor. Serve with white rice.

6 chicken breasts, skinned & boned
salt and pepper
2 T. vegetable oil
1/4 cup butter
1 onion, thinly sliced
2 cloves garlic, minced

15 canned green chilies
1/2 cup milk
1/2 tsp. salt
1 cup sour cream
1 cup shredded Cheddar cheese

Season the chicken with salt and pepper. Heat oil and butter in skillet, add chicken and saute until lightly browned. Remove from skillet. In the same skillet, fry the onion and garlic about 5 minutes. Take 10 of the chilies and cut them into strips. Add them to the onion, cover and cook 5 minutes. Season with salt and pepper. Process the milk, the remaining 5 chilies and salt in a blender until smooth. Add the sour cream and blend a few more seconds.

Arrange the chicken in an ovenproof dish. Cover with the onion/chile mixture and top with the sour cream sauce. Sprinkle cheese on top and bake in a 350° oven about 30 minutes.

Chicken in Green Sauce

For an enchilada dish, wrap the chicken (moistened with some sauce) in tortillas. Top with green sauce and cheese. Garnish with sour cream.

2 to 2-1/2 lb. chicken
3 celery stalks, cut into chunks
1 onion, cut into chunks
salt and pepper

Green sauce (page 134), doubled
1-1/2 cups shredded Jack cheese

Vegetables:
2 T. butter
2 green peppers, diced
2 onions, diced
2 large tomatoes, diced
3 Anaheim chiles, roasted, peeled & diced
salt and pepper

Garnish: sour cream, black olives

Place chicken in dutch oven with the celery, onion, salt and pepper. Add water to cover and simmer until tender, about 40 minutes. Let cool, remove meat from the bones and shred.

Vegetables: Combine all the ingredients in a large skillet. Cook until soft. Add the shredded chicken and green sauce and mix well. Taste for seasoning.

Place in an ovenproof dish, top with cheese and bake in a 350° oven for 20 minutes or until cheese is melted. Garnish with sour cream and black olives.

Baked Chili Chicken

Serves 6

Chicken, marinated in an aromatic sauce, and then baked. The sour cream smoothes out the wonderful flavors.

6 chicken breasts
1 stick butter
1/2 tsp. cumin
6 T. chili powder
1/8 tsp. ground cloves
2 cloves garlic, minced
1 T. flour
salt and pepper
sour cream

Melt the butter in a skillet and add the cumin, chili powder, cloves and garlic. Stir for about 2-3 minutes. Stir in the flour. Coat the chicken with the sauce and place in a baking dish. Pour the remaining sauce over the chicken and marinate in refrigerator at least 3 hours.

Bake, uncovered in a 350° oven about 45 minutes. Baste occasionally.

Place chicken on a serving platter. Add the sour cream to juices in pan until sauce has consistency you prefer. Heat through and serve with chicken.

Mole de Pollo

The most famous national dish of Mexico. Traditionally made of turkey. Here we will use chicken in this spicy sauce of chilies, nuts, spices, herbs and a bit of chocolate. Serve with rice.

1/2 cup lard or shortening
1/4 cup chili powder
2 cups chicken broth
2 corn tortillas, cut in pieces
2 flour tortillas, cut in pieces
2 tomatoes, diced
1 onion, chopped
2 cloves garlic, minced
2 T. raisins
2 T. almonds
2 T. peanuts
2 T. sesame seeds

1 T. sugar
1 tsp. oregano
1/2 tsp. thyme
1 bay leaf
3/4 oz. Mexican chocolate
   (or 1 T. unsweetened cocoa)
1/2 tsp. ground cinnamon
1/2 tsp. ground cloves
1/2 tsp. cumin
1/2 tsp. allspice
2 cups chicken broth
8 chicken breasts, boned

Heat the lard in a large skillet until very hot. Stir in the chili powder and cook until brown. Stir in the remaining ingredients except the second 2 cups of chicken broth and chicken. Simmer for 1 hour. Let cool.

Pour some of the sauce into a blender. Puree until smooth. Continue with the remaining sauce.

Heat the sauce and remaining 2 cups chicken broth in a skillet. Place the chicken in the sauce and simmer for one hour or until chicken is tender.

Baked Chicken with Tomatillo Rice

Golden chicken pieces atop rice flavored with tomatillos and chilies.

4 large chicken breasts, skinned and boned
2 T. vegetable oil
1 onion, chopped
2 cloves garlic, minced
1 cup uncooked, long grain white rice
1-1/2 lbs. tomatillos, cooked
1 (4 oz) can green chilies, sliced
1 tsp. cumin
1/4 cup chopped cilantro
2 cups chicken broth

Heat oil in a large skillet and brown the chicken. Remove and set aside. Add the onion, garlic and rice to the skillet. Cook until rice is a golden brown, about 15 minutes. Add the remaining ingredients and mix well. Transfer to a baking dish, place chicken on top. Cover and bake in a 350° oven for 45 minutes.

Charcoal-Grilled Chicken

Chicken, marinated in a mild, garlicky sauce, and then charcoal grilled. Serve with charro beans, a salad and corn tortillas. For variation, you might want to try with cornish game hens.

2 chickens, cut into serving pieces
Marinade:
1 onion, chopped
6 cloves garlic, chopped
1-1/2 cups fresh orange juice
1 tsp. oregano
1/2 tsp. thyme
3 bay leaves
salt and pepper

Place all the marinade ingredients in a blender and puree. Place the chicken in a glass bowl and coat thoroughly with the marinade. Cover and refrigerate overnight. Turn chicken occasionally.

Grill the chicken about 45 minutes, turning and basting with the marinade.

Chicken in Pumpkin Seed Sauce

Serves 4

Chicken, cooked in a unique pale-green sauce similar to a green mole or pipian verde. Traditionally served with a sparkling limeade to drink.

6 chicken breasts
1 tsp. salt
1 onion, sliced
1 cup pumpkin seeds (pepitas)
1 cup chicken broth
8 tomatillos, cooked
2 chiles serranos, chopped
1 chile jalapeno, chopped
5 lettuce leaves

1/2 onion, chopped
2 cloves garlic, minced
2 T. chopped cilantro
1/4 tsp. cumin
3/4 tsp. ground cinnamon
1/8 tsp. ground cloves
2 T. lard or shortening
2 cups chicken broth
salt and pepper

In a large saucepan, cover the chicken with water. Add the salt and onion. Simmer for 15 minutes. Remove chicken and set aside.

Heat a skillet and toast the pumpkin seeds until they pop. Cool. Grind in a blender and add 1 cup chicken broth. Remove and set aside.

Puree the tomatillos and chilies in blender. Add the lettuce, onion, garlic, cilantro and spices. Process until smooth.

Heat the lard in a large skillet and add the pumpkin seed/broth mixture. Stir constantly until it thickens, about 5 minutes. Add the vegetable puree and stir until very thick. Add 2 cups chicken broth and simmer 30 minutes. Season with salt and pepper. Add more broth if necessary. Add the chicken to the sauce and heat thoroughly.

Orange Chicken

A fantastic orangey flavor with aromatic spices and full of raisins, capers and almonds.

4 chicken breasts
1/8 tsp. ground cinnamon
1/8 tsp. ground cloves
salt and pepper, to taste
1/4 cup vegetable oil
2 cloves garlic, minced

1 onion, chopped
1 cup fresh orange juice
2 T. seedless raisins
1 T. capers
1/2 cup slivered almonds
Garnish: orange wedges

Combine cinnamon, cloves, salt and pepper in small bowl and sprinkle over the chicken. Heat oil in skillet, add chicken and brown. Remove from skillet and set aside. Saute the garlic and onion for 5 minutes in the same skillet. Return the chicken and add the orange juice, raisins and capers. Cook until done, about 45 minutes. Stir in the almonds just before serving.

Garnish with orange wedges.

Chicken Cilantro

A wonderful dish with the fresh taste of cilantro and lemon.

4 T. butter
2 T. vegetable oil
1 onion, chopped
2 cloves garlic, minced
6 chicken breasts, boned, skinned, and cut in 1" pieces
1/4 cup chopped cilantro
2 T. lemon juice
salt and pepper
Garnish:
lemon wedges

Heat butter and oil in large skillet, add onion and garlic and saute about 5 minutes. Add the chicken. Stirring occasionally, cook about 10 minutes, or until tender.
Stir in the cilantro and lemon juice. Cook another 2 minutes.
Garnish with lemon wedges.

Chicken Fruit Stew

A chicken stew enriched with fruit which is popular throughout Central Mexico. All you need to serve with this are hot tortillas and pickled jalapenos.

6 chicken breasts
6 chicken thighs
salt
1/2 tsp. freshly ground pepper
pinch of ground cloves
1/8 tsp. ground cinnamon
1 T. sugar
1/4 cup dry Sherry
3 cloves garlic, minced

1/4 cup apple cider vinegar
1-1/2 tsp. salt
1 onion, sliced
2 tomatoes, sliced
1 tart apple, cored & sliced
1 pear, cored & sliced
2 bay leaves
1/4 tsp. thyme
1/4 tsp. oregano

Garnish:
2 T. capers
2 plantains or bananas, peeled, sliced & fried in butter

Sprinkle the chicken pieces with salt. Mix together in a bowl the pepper, cloves, cinnamon, sugar, sherry, garlic, vinegar and salt. Layer half the onion, tomatoes, fruit and herbs in the bottom of an ovenproof casserole. Place the chicken pieces on top and pour on the vinegar/spice mixture. Top with the remaining half of the onion, tomatoes, fruit and herbs. Cover and bake in a 375° oven for 1 hour. Uncover and bake another 30 minutes.

To serve, garnish with fried plantains and capers.

Seafood

With its 6,000 miles of seashore, Mexico offers an abundance of the freshest fish and shellfish. Even landlocked Mexicans have endless varieties to choose from.

The Spaniards contributed their own special seasonings and ingredients to help create some outstanding Mexican fish dishes.

Use your judgement when determining the "doneness" of fish. The rule of thumb is ten minutes for each inch of thickness. It is done if it flakes **easily** and / or separates from the bone. If you prefer your fish moister, cook until it flakes under gentle but **firm pressure**.

Red Snapper Veracruz

The mention of Mexican seafood, brings to mind this colorful dish with its chunky tomato sauce with olives, herbs and chilies. It has many variations - this is my favorite. White rice is a good accompaniment.

1-1/2 lbs. red snapper or halibut fillets
1 tsp. salt
2 T. lime juice
3 T. olive oil
1 onion, thinly sliced
3 cloves garlic, minced
2 lbs. tomatoes, skinned & seeded
1 bay leaf

1/2 tsp. oregano
12 pitted green olives, halved
2 T. capers
2 chilies jalapenos
salt and pepper
1 tsp. cumin
1/4 cup dry white wine

Prick the fish on both sides with a fork. Place in a glass baking dish. Sprinkle with the salt and lime juice. Refrigerate 2 hours.

Heat olive oil in large skillet and saute onion and garlic until soft. Add the tomatoes and remaining ingredients. Simmer about 15 minutes. Pour sauce over the fish and bake, uncovered in a 325° oven about 45 minutes or until fish is cooked. Baste frequently with the sauce.

Red Snapper in Sour Cream Sauce

Fish fillets topped with a savory blend of chilies, mushrooms and sour cream and topped with cheese.

3 T. butter
3 T. flour
2 cups sour cream
1 cup half and half
1 clove garlic, minced
salt and pepper

3 lbs. red snapper fillets
6 T. butter
12 mushrooms, sliced
6 Anaheim chilies, roasted, stemmed
    and seeded
1 cup shredded Jack cheese
1 cup shredded Cheddar cheese

Melt butter in saucepan. Whisk in flour. Cook 1 minute. Then whisk in sour cream and half and half. Add garlic, salt and pepper. Simmer 10 minutes.

Place red snapper in a baking dish.

Melt the 6 T. butter in a skillet. Saute the mushrooms and chilies about 5 minutes. Drain and spoon over fish. Top with sour cream mixture, sprinkle with cheese. Bake in 350° oven about 25 minutes.

Halibut in Citrus Sauce

Serves 4

A tangy lemon-orange sauce makes this a wonderful dish for warm summer evenings. You can use any firm-fleshed fish such as red snapper, cod or pompano.

2 lbs. halibut fillets
salt and pepper
2 T. minced cilantro
2 cloves garlic, minced
1/4 tsp. cumin
2 T. olive oil
juice of 1 lemon
juice of 3 oranges

Sprinkle fish with salt and pepper. Place in glass baking dish. Combine remaining ingredients in bowl and pour over fish. Refrigerate one hour.

Bake in a 350° oven about 30 minutes or until fish flakes. Baste often during cooking.

Sea Bass in Pecan Sauce

Poached fish with a smooth pecan sauce. You can substitute any firm-textured mild fish.

1 cup dry white wine
1/2 cup water
1 bay leaf
1/2 tsp. salt
4 whole peppercorns
2 lbs. seabass fillets
1 onion, sliced
2 cloves garlic

1/2 cup pecans
2 T. parsley
1/4 tsp. saffron
salt
1/4 tsp. ground mild red chile
juice of 1 lemon
Garnish:
lemon wedges

In large skillet combine the first 5 ingredients. Simmer 10 minutes. Add the fish and simmer until fish flakes. Place fish on a serving platter. Remove the peppercorns and bayleaf from the liquid, then pour into a blender. Add the remaining ingredients and blend until smooth. Spoon sauce over fish. Garnish with lemon wedges.

Grilled Swordfish with Cilantro-Butter Sauce

Serves 4

The lime juice marinade, charcoal grilling, and basting with pungent cilantro-butter makes this a Mexican masterpiece.

2 lbs. swordfish steaks
3 T. fresh lime juice
salt and pepper

Cilantro Butter Sauce:
1 stick butter
1 clove garlic, minced
3/4 cup chopped cilantro
1 serrano chile, minced

Garnish:
lime wedges

In a glass bowl, marinate swordfish in lime, salt and pepper 2 hours. Grill until just opaque, about 6 minutes per side. Baste with cilantro butter. Serve with lime wedges.

Cilantro Butter: Melt butter in skillet. Saute garlic 1 minute. Add cilantro and chile. Heat through.

Paella

This seafood classic is one of Spain's contributions to the cuisine of Mexico. Ingredients vary from region to region. You can vary according to your taste.

4 bacon strips, diced
1/2 cup chorizo (page 18),
   rolled in small balls
1/2 lb. lean pork, cubed
2 chicken breasts, cubed
1/2 cup ham, cubed
3 celery stalks, chopped
8 artichoke hearts, halved
2 large tomatoes, peeled & quartered
3 cloves garlic
3 canned chipotle chilies
1/2 onion, chopped

2 cups uncooked long grain white rice
4 cups boiling water
1/2 tsp. saffron
8 clams in the shell
1/2 cup crab
1/2 lb. raw shrimp, peeled & deveined
8 mussels in the shell
Garnish:
4 hard cooked eggs, halved
1/3 cup sliced ripe olives
1/2 cup chopped parsley

In large skillet, brown the bacon and chorizo. Remove to large dutch oven. Discard all but 4 tablespoons of fat. Add the pork, chicken, and ham and brown. Then mix with the chorizo in dutch oven. Saute the celery and artichoke hearts 5 minutes and add to pot.

In a blender, puree the tomatoes, garlic, chilies and onion. Fry this mixture in the skillet for 5 minutes. Pour over the meat and vegetables. Add the rice, boiling water and saffron. Cover pot and steam over low heat for 30 minutes. Add the seafood the last 5 minutes.

Arrange paella on a platter and garnish with eggs, olives and parsley.

Shrimp in Pumpkin Seed Sauce

Serves 4

A elegant and unusual dish. The shrimp will be more tender and flavorful if cooked in their shells.

1-1/2 lbs. medium shrimp, unshelled
water
1/2 tsp. salt
4 peppercorns
1 bayleaf
1 cup (4 oz) pumpkin seeds (pepitas)
1-1/2 cups clam juice
1 T. cilantro
1 chile serrano, chopped
1 chile jalapeno, chopped
1/2 white onion
1 T. butter
1 cup sour cream

In a saucepan, place the shrimp, enough water to cover them, and the salt, peppercorns and bayleaf. Simmer about 3 minutes or until shrimp turn pink. Remove shrimp, let cool, then shell and devein.

In a skillet, toast the seeds until they start to pop. Add clam juice, cilantro, chilies, onion and seeds to blender. Puree until smooth. Melt butter in skillet and add sauce. Cook over low heat 10 minutes. Stir in shrimp. Remove from heat and add sour cream. Return to heat until just heated through. Thin with water if necessary.

good!

Prawns in Garlic Butter

Serves 4

A wonderful presentation for prawns - simply sauteed in garlic butter and olive oil.

1/2 stick butter
1/4 cup olive oil
8 cloves garlic, minced
2 lbs. raw prawns (or large shrimp), peeled & deveined
salt and pepper
2 T. lemon juice
Garnish:
lemon wedges
chopped parsley

Melt the butter with the olive oil in a skillet. Add the garlic and prawns. Sprinkle with salt and pepper. Add lemon juice. Saute until prawns turn pink, only about 3-4 minutes. Turn and cook other side.

Garnish with lemon wedges and parsley.

Shrimp in Bell Pepper Cream Sauce

Serves 4

An intriguing flavor with cilantro and tequila highlighting a cream sauce with bell peppers.

3 T. butter
3 red bell peppers, cut in slivers
3 green bell peppers, cut in slivers
1 stick butter
2 tsp. lemon juice
2 cloves garlic, minced

2 T. dry white wine
salt and pepper
20 large shrimp, peeled & deveined
1/2 cup tequila
1-1/2 cups heavy cream
1/4 cup chopped cilantro

Melt 3 T. of the butter in a skillet and saute the bell peppers until tender. Remove peppers from skillet and set aside.

Melt the 1 stick butter in same skillet and add the lemon juice, garlic and wine. Cook 5 minutes. Season with salt and pepper. Add the shrimp and cook about 3 minutes. Add the tequila, heat and ignite with match. When flame subsides, remove shrimp. Add cream and boil until thickened. Return shrimp along with bell peppers and cilantro and heat through.

Broiled Shrimp with Tomatillo Relish

Serves 6

Beautiful pink grilled shrimp top a cool, tart green relish of tomatillos.

3 cups dry white wine
2/3 cup olive oil
1/2 white onion, chopped
4 cloves garlic, minced
1 T. black peppercorns

30 large shrimp, shelled & deveined

Tomatillo Relish:
1-1/2 lbs. tomatillos, cooked & pureed
3/4 cup vinegar
3 tomatoes, chopped
2 Anaheim chilies, roasted & diced
2 jalapeno peppers, diced
3 T. olive oil
2 tsp. basil
1 tsp. oregano
salt and pepper

In glass bowl combine first 5 ingredients. Add shrimp and toss to coat. Cover and refrigerate overnight.

Grill or broil the shrimp about 3 minutes per side. Spoon relish on a platter and top with shrimp.

Relish: Combine all ingredients in glass bowl. Cover and refrigerate at least 3 hours. Serve at room temperature.

Almond Coated Shrimp

The Mexican version of deep-fried shrimp, coated with a batter and dipped in crushed almonds. Butterfly the shrimp if you wish.

3 eggs
1/3 cup half and half
3/4 cup flour
3 cloves garlic, minced
2 lbs. large shrimp, shelled and deveined
1-1/2 cups crushed almonds
vegetable oil
Garnish:
lime wedges

In a bowl beat the eggs, half and half, flour and garlic together for the batter. Dip each shrimp in batter and then roll in almonds. Set shrimp on a baking sheet and refrigerate 30 minutes.

Heat oil in deep frying pan or deep fat fryer to 375.° Fry the shrimp until golden. Drain on paper towels.

Garnish with lime wedges.

Shrimp with Toasted Garlic and Avocado

Serves 4

Shrimp marinated in toasted garlic oil and then charcoal grilled and topped with avocado mayonnaise.

6 T. olive oil
10 cloves garlic, thinly sliced
2 T. fresh lime juice
salt
2 lbs. large shrimp, peeled & deveined

Heat olive oil in skillet and saute the garlic slowly until golden, about 4 minutes. Discard the garlic. In glass bowl combine the oil, lime juice, salt and shrimp. Marinate overnight.
Charcoal grill the shrimp about 3 minutes per side. Serve with avocado mayonnaise.

Avocado Mayonnaise:

1 avocado, peeled & chopped
1/3 cup fresh lime juice
1 egg
1/2 cup parsley
1/2 cup beer
1/2 small onion, chopped
1-1/2 cups olive oil
salt

   Avocado Mayonnaise: Place avocado, lime juice, egg, parsley, beer and onion in blender. Puree. Then **slowly** add olive oil. Season with salt.

Vegetables, Beans and Rice

Beans are essential to a Mexican meal. They are by far the most popular vegetable in Mexico, with corn and rice as close seconds.

Rice was brought to Mexico by the Spaniards. It is typically served as a sopa seca or ''dry soup'' course in the midday comida.

Squashes, chilies, potatoes, greens, tomatoes, and mushrooms are blended together with various cheeses and seasonings to create a vegetable side dish. They usually are not served alone, but are joined by meats and poultry for a main entree.

Chilies with Cheese

A chili con queso dish eaten with broiled meats or as an appetizer with hot tortillas. Use the canned chilies or 20 fresh Anaheim chilies roasted and peeled.

3 T. vegetable oil
1 onion, thinly sliced
2 medium tomatoes, thinly sliced
1 (27 oz) can whole chilies, cut into strips
3/4 cup milk
1/2 lb. mild Cheddar or Muenster cheese, shredded
salt

Heat oil in skillet and cook the onion until soft. Add the tomatoes and chilies. Cook about 10 minutes. Add the milk and cook a few minutes.
Stir in the cheese and salt. Serve as soon as the cheese melts.

Potatoes and Chilies

   A good side dish for any meat dish.

3 T. bacon fat
1 large onion, chopped
4 potatoes, diced
salt
1 cup chopped green chilies

   Heat the bacon fat in a skillet. Saute the onion until soft. Add potatoes and fry until golden. Add the salt and chilies. Stir and cook another 3 minutes.

Corn and Zucchini - Mexican Style

Serves 4

The yellow, green and red vegetables make this a dish true to the Mexican style and flair for color.

1 onion, thinly sliced
1 clove garlic, minced
3 T. olive oil
1/2 lb. zucchini, sliced
1 green pepper, julienned
2 cups of corn kernels (about 4 ears)
1-1/2 cups chopped tomatoes
1-1/2 tsp. chili powder
salt and pepper
1/3 cup shredded Cheddar cheese

Heat olive oil in a skillet and saute onion and garlic until soft. Add the zucchini and green pepper. Saute them for 3 minutes. Add the corn, tomatoes, chili powder, salt and pepper. Pour into a buttered baking dish. Cover and bake in a 350° oven for 15 minutes. Sprinkle with cheese and bake 10 minutes or until cheese is melted.

Tomatoes Stuffed with Corn Pudding

For a variation, add cooked bacon and / or shredded cheese to the corn pudding.

8 medium tomatoes
salt and pepper
2 eggs, room temperature
2 T. flour
1 T. sugar
1/2 tsp. baking powder
1 cup half and half
1 cup corn kernels
2 T. butter, melted
Garnish:
chopped parsley

Slice the tops off the tomatoes. Scoop out pulp. Sprinkle with salt and pepper and invert on paper towels for 20 minutes to drain.

Beat the eggs in a medium bowl. Blend in the remaining ingredients. Season with salt and pepper. Spoon into tomatoes. Place on baking sheet. Bake in a 350° oven until puffed, lightly browned and firm - about 45 minutes. Garnish with chopped parsley.

Chili-Stuffed Squash

Serves 4

The pretty green scalloped-edge pattypan squash is filled with a creamy chili mixture.

2 T. butter
8 pattypan squash
8 oz. cream cheese, room temperature
3 T. chopped green chilies
2 T. half and half
salt and pepper
dash of hot pepper sauce
1/2 cup shredded Monterey Jack cheese

Butter a baking dish with the 2 T. of butter. Scoop out the center of squash to leave a form shell. Combine the remaining ingredients, except Jack cheese, in a bowl and blend well. Spoon into the squash. Place in the baking dish. Cover and bake in a 350° oven for 30-45 minutes or until tender.

Sprinkle with cheese and place under the broiler until cheese is golden brown.

Green Beans with Lime and Chilies

Serves 6

Lime juice is often the touch that transforms a dish to "Mexican." Add cilantro and chilies and it's really authentic.

1-1/2 lbs. fresh green beans, cut in 2" lengths
1/2 stick butter
3 T. fresh lime juice
1/4 cup chopped cilantro
2 serrano chiles, minced
salt and pepper

Bring water in a saucepan to a boil. Add the beans and cook until crisp-tender. Cool immediately in ice water. Drain.

To serve, melt the butter in a skillet. Add the beans and remaining ingredients and heat thoroughly.

Green Beans and Tomatoes

A very colorful dish with a wonderful flavor.

1 lb. fresh green beans, cut in 2" lengths
4 slices bacon, diced
1 small onion, chopped
2 cloves garlic, minced
1 tomato, diced
1 tsp. oregano
salt and pepper
2 T. fresh lemon juice

Bring water to boil in a saucepan. Add beans and cook until crisp-tender. Immediately cool in ice water. Drain.

Fry the bacon in a skillet. When crisp, remove from skillet. Cook the onion and garlic in the bacon fat until soft, about 5 minutes. Add the tomato, oregano, salt and pepper. Simmer 10 minutes. Stir in the beans, lemon juice and bacon bits. Heat thoroughly.

Mushrooms in Green Sauce

A very attractive and unusual way to serve mushrooms.

2 T. vegetable oil
1/2 white onion, chopped
1/2 lb. mushrooms, sliced
2 jalapeno chiles
1/4 tsp. cumin
8 tomatillos, cooked
1 clove garlic, minced
salt and pepper

Heat oil in a skillet and saute the onion until soft. Add the mushrooms and chilies and cook for another 2 minutes. Add the remaining ingredients, cover and simmer 15 minutes to blend the flavors.

Marinated-Broiled Onions

Serves 4

Sweet red onions, broiled and then marinated in olive oil and lime. Served on a bed of lettuce, it is an artful complement to meat dishes.

2 large red onions, cut into 1/2" thick slices
olive oil
pepper
2 T. olive oil
3 tsp. fresh lime juice
1/2 tsp. oregano
salt

Place the onions on a broiler pan. Brush with olive oil and sprinkle with pepper. Broil about 8 minutes or until soft and beginning to char. Turn over and broil another 2 minutes.

Place in a glass bowl. Add the remaining ingredients. Let stand 2-3 hours before serving.

Chiles Rellenos de Queso

Serves 4

Fresh chiles, stuffed with cheese (or meat), coated with an egg batter, and fried golden brown. Served with a tomato sauce, for those who desire.

8 poblano chiles
2 cups shredded Monterey Jack cheese
1 cup dry breadcrumbs
4 eggs, separated
1/4 tsp. salt
vegetable oil
Mexican Red Sauce (page 131), thinned with some water
Garnish:
chopped cilantro
sour cream

Chili Rellenos
(New Mexican)
8 whole green chilis
fresh or canned seeds removed)
Monterey Jack or cheddar
cheese, cut in sticks.
Flour for dredging
4 eggs, separated
2 tsp. baking powder
1 tbsp water
1/4 tsp salt

Stuff chilis & pat dry. Beat egg
whites until stiff. Combine
remaining ingred. & gently fold
them into egg whites to make a
batter. Roll stuffed chilis in
flour & carefully dip them in the
batter & coat well. Deep fry the
chilis, turning constantly until

Broil the chilies 4-5 minutes each side until skin blisters. Wrap in a towel and let stand for 5 minutes. Peel the skin off carefully. Cut a slit lengthwise in each. Remove seeds and membranes. Fill with 1/4 cup cheese. Coat with breadcrumbs and refrigerate 20 minutes.

In a bowl beat the egg whites until stiff. In another bowl beat the yolks and salt until thick and lemon-colored. Fold into the whites. Heat 1/2" of oil in a skillet. Dip the peppers in the egg mixture and fry, one by one, until puffy and golden, about 3 minutes. Drain on paper towels.

Serve plain or with Mexican Red Sauce. Garnish with chopped cilantro and sour cream.

Chili Rellenos Casserole

Line baking dish with the stuffed chilis, pour batter over the top, & bake 40 mins at 350°F. Pour sauce over top before serving.

lightly browned.
Remove & drain.
Top with chili sauce,
rice & beans.
Can be stuffed with meats
& cheese.

Picadillo Filling for Chiles Rellenos

This is another choice for filling Chiles Rellenos on the preceding page. Use this instead of the cheese.

1/2 lb. beef, coarsely ground
1/2 onion, chopped
2 cloves garlic, minced
2 tomatoes, diced
1/4 cup seedless raisins
1/2 tsp. salt
1 carrot, diced
1 potato, diced
1/2 tsp. grated lemon peel
2 T. slivered almonds

In a skillet brown the meat and add the onion and garlic. Add the remaining ingredients except almonds. Simmer 30 minutes. Add almonds.

Stuff the prepared chilies and proceed with the batter and frying (see page 112).

Arroz a la Mexicana

The flavors of nutty browned rice and tomato - classic Mexican flavors.

1 garlic clove, minced
2 T. vegetable oil
1 cup uncooked long grain rice
2 cups chicken broth
1/2 cup Mexican Red Sauce (page 131)

In a large saucepan, saute the garlic in the oil for 2-3 minutes. Stir in the rice and cook until lightly browned, about 5 minutes. Stir in the chicken broth and Mexican Red Sauce. Bring to a boil, then reduce the heat. Cover and simmer 20 minutes. Do not lift cover or stir.

Rice with Raisins and Almonds

Serves 4

A sweet rice dish which goes well with picadillo, mole or seafood.

2 cups water
3/4 tsp. salt
1 cup uncooked long grain rice
1/2 tsp. sugar
1 T. butter
1/3 cup seedless raisins
1/2 cup slivered almonds

In a saucepan bring water, salt and rice to a boil. Cover and simmer 20 minutes or until the rice is done.

Add the remaining ingredients and warm for 2 minutes.

Arroz Verde

While red rice gets made every day, green rice is a Holiday rice dish.

1-1/2 cups uncooked long grain
    white rice
1/3 cup vegetable oil
1/2 cup water
6 sprigs parsley
2 T. chopped cilantro

3 large Romaine lettuce leaves
2 peeled (canned) green chilies
3 scallions
1 garlic clove
3 cups chicken broth
salt, to taste

In a saucepan fry the rice in the oil over high heat until it is a golden color. Drain off most of the oil.

Put in a blender the water, parsley, cilantro, lettuce, chilies, scallions and garlic. Blend until smooth. Add this mixture to the rice and cook over high heat until the rice is almost dry. Add the chicken broth and salt to taste. Cook on medium heat until small air holes appear in the surface of the rice, about 15 minutes. Cover and cook another 5 minutes, then turn off the heat and let the rice continue cooking in its own steam for 20-30 minutes.

Black Beans

Serves 8

The bean of Southern, Gulf Coastal and Yucatan Mexico. Often stewed with a sprig of epazote, a pungent jaggered-leaf herb / weed.

4 cups water
1 lb. dried black beans
1 medium onion, chopped
1/2 cup vegetable oil
3 garlic cloves, minced
2 slices bacon, diced
1 tsp. cumin
1 T. chili powder
1/2 cup minced cilantro (optional)
1 tsp. salt

Mix water, beans and onion in a stockpot. Cover and heat to boiling. Boil about 2 minutes. Remove from heat and let stand 1 hour.

Add just enough water to the beans to cover. Stir in the oil, garlic, bacon, cumin, chili powder and cilantro. Heat to boiling. Reduce heat, cover and simmer until beans are very tender, about 2 hours. Add the salt and mix well. Drain and serve.

Pinto Beans

The popular bean in Northern Mexico - it has a light brown color and a wonderful rich flavor. Serve as is and / or use for refried beans.

1 lb. dried pinto beans
1/2 lb. bacon, cut into 1" pieces
1 medium tomato, diced
1 T. cumin
1 T. chili powder
2 garlic cloves, minced
1 serrano chili, minced
salt, to taste

Place beans in large saucepan. Cover with water and bring to a boil. Drain, return beans to pan. Cover with water by 2 inches. Add all ingredients except salt. Boil, reduce heat and simmer until beans are done, about 3-1/2 hours. Add salt to taste and cook another 15 minutes.

Refried Beans

The real translation for these frijoles refritos are **well** fried beans. A national side dish.

4 T. bacon fat or lard
4 cups cooked pinto beans (page 119)
2 cloves garlic, minced
salt
3/4 cup shredded Monterey Jack cheese

In a skillet heat bacon fat. Add the beans and a bit of the liquid. Mash them until thoroughly crushed. Add the garlic and season with salt.

Cook over low heat about 20 minutes. Sprinkle cheese on top and continue heating until melted.

Frijoles a la Charra

Served in their broth in small soup bowls. Literal translation means beans cooked the way the lady charro (elegant horseman) would prepare them.

1/4 lb. salt pork
1/2 lb. pinto beans
1/2 onion, sliced
2 garlic cloves, minced
6 cups water

1-1/4 tsp. salt
1/4 lb. bacon, diced
2 tomatoes, peeled, seeded & chopped
3 chiles serranos, minced
2 T. chopped cilantro

Place the first 5 ingredients in a dutch oven and bring to a boil. Lower the heat, cover and simmer gently until beans are tender, about 1-1/2 hours. Add the salt and cook, uncovered, for another 15 minutes.

Cook the bacon in a skillet until slightly browned. Add the remaining ingredients and cook over high heat for 10 minutes. Add the tomato mixture to the beans and let cook together, uncovered, over low heat for about 15 minutes.

Salads and Sauces

Unlike beans, a salad is rarely seen as an essential part of a Mexican meal. Lettuce is used more as a mere garnish to the dish. In fact, raw vegetables on the whole are mostly used as an accompaniment to the course, instead of by themselves.

Sauces, on the other hand, are a must on any Mexican table. Chilies are the key ingredient in many sauces, but with bountiful variations. What contrast a Mexican cook can achieve when concocting different sauces, from gentle tomato sauces to a fiery blend of red hot chilies. You can also add a special tartness with green sauces by using small tomatillos.

There is no end to the variety of sauces.

Chicken, meat & pork.
1 med. onion finely chopped.
2 tbsp. salad oil.
2 cans (10 oz each) tomatillos
about 3 tbsp minced canned
    cal. green chilis
2 C. regular strength chicken
    broth.

Green Tomatillo Sauce
a thick meat sauce to serve with
1/4 C finely chopped blanched almonds
1 tbsp. minced cilantro
Combine onion, almonds & oil, & cook,
stirring over mod. heat until onion is
soft & almonds lightly browned.
Whirl the tomatillos in blender until
fairly smooth. Add to onions etc. Stir
in coriander & chilis. Sauce should be
fairly mild. Add the chicken broth &
simmer rapidly, uncovered, until
reduced to 2½ cups. Stir occasionally
Keeps several days.

Pico di Gallo

The name "rooster's beak" refers to the old style of eating salad by picking up the chunks with your fingers, the way a rooster pecks corn. This version is served as a salad or a sauce.

2 avocados, peeled, seeded and mashed
1/2 onion, chopped
1 tomato, diced
2 serrano chiles, minced
2 tsp. fresh lemon juice
1 T. minced cilantro
1/2 tsp. garlic salt
1/2 tsp. oregano

Combine all the ingredients together in a small bowl. Serve on a bed of lettuce as a salad or as a sauce.

Pinto Bean Salad

A good way to use leftover pinto beans. Or, a good reason to cook a pot of beans.

2 cups cooked pinto beans
3 celery stalks, diced
3 T. minced onion
3 T. chopped parsley
1 T. cumin
1/4 cup mayonnaise
1/4 cup vegetable oil
2 T. fresh lime juice
salt and pepper

Toss all the ingredients together in a bowl. Cover and refrigerate 2 hours.

Jicama Salad

Spicy Mexican dishes benefit from a crunchy, cooling salad companion. Jicama is a tropical root vegetable with a crisp, fresh flavor.

1 red onion, thinly sliced
salted water
red leaf or butter lettuce
1-1/2 cups jicama, peeled and julienned
Dressing:
3 T. fresh lemon juice
2 T. fresh lime juice
1/4 tsp. salt
1 cup olive or vegetable oil

Soak the red onion in salted water for 2 hours. Drain. Arrange lettuce on a platter. Top lettuce with onion and jicama. Combine the dressing ingredients in a small bowl. Pour over the salad and mix gently.

Salads & Sauces 125

Christmas Eve Salad

After Christmas Eve mass, this salad is served at a supper with a classic turkey dish.

1 head Romaine lettuce
3 oranges, peeled & sectioned
2 firm bananas, sliced
2 apples, cored & sliced
2 cups pineapple chunks
1 lime, thinly sliced
1 cup shoestring beets
1/2 cup salted peanuts
1/2 cup seedless raisins

Dressing:
1/4 cup vinegar
1 T. lime juice
3 T. orange juice
2/3 cup vegetable oil
salt and pepper
1 tsp. sugar

Place lettuce leaves in a large bowl. Arrange remaining ingredients on top of lettuce. Combine dressing ingredients in small bowl and pour over the salad.

Cauliflower and Avocado Salad

Serves 6

Marinated cauliflower, on a bed of lettuce, topped with a luscious green avocado dressing.

1 head cauliflower, separated into florets
3 T. vinegar
3 T. vegetable oil
salt and pepper
lettuce - Romaine, butter or red leaf
Guacamole (page 15)
Garnish:
3 T. slivered almonds

Bring water to boil in a saucepan. Add cauliflower florets and cook for 4 minutes. Rinse in ice water and drain. In a bowl, combine the vinegar, oil, salt and pepper. Add the cauliflower, toss and refrigerate 2 hours.

Arrange the cauliflower on lettuce lined plates. Top with the guacamole and garnish with almonds.

Pickled Coleslaw

A Mexican version of our coleslaw. This will keep for several days in the refrigerator.

1 cup vegetable oil
1 cup cider vinegar
1-1/4 cups sugar
2 T. celery seeds
3 lbs. cabbage, chopped
1 green pepper, chopped
2 white onions, finely chopped
1 T. salt
1/2 tsp. freshly ground pepper

In a saucepan heat the oil, vinegar, sugar and celery seeds until the mixture boils and the sugar dissolves. Simmer for a few minutes.

Combine the vegetables in a large bowl. Season with salt and pepper. Pour the hot dressing over the vegetables. Let stand for at least 2 hours before serving.

   Acapulco Chicken Enchiladas (page 48) ➠

Orange-Onion-Avocado Salad

Attractive rows of oranges, onions and avocado spiced with chili powder in the dressing.

lettuce
3 large oranges, peeled and sectioned
1 red onion, thinly sliced
2 avocados, peeled, pitted and sliced
Dressing:
1/3 cup vegetable oil
1/4 cup vinegar
1 tsp. sugar
salt
1/2 tsp. chili powder

Arrange the lettuce on a platter. Layer the oranges, onion and avocados in overlapping rows. Mix the dressing ingredients together in a bowl and spoon over the salad.

Orange Salad with Pecan Dressing

When the word "neuz" is used by Mexicans, it commonly refers to the native pecan. The addition of pecans makes a very interesting dressing for this salad.

4 oranges, peeled and sectioned
1 head lettuce, torn into bite size pieces
Dressing:
1/4 cup ground pecans
2 T. mayonnaise
2 T. sour cream
1 T. fresh lime juice
1/2 tsp. sugar
1/2 tsp. salt
1/8 tsp. cinnamon
freshly ground pepper, to taste

Place the orange sections in a bowl with the lettuce. Mix the dressing ingredients in a bowl and pour over the oranges and lettuce. Toss and serve.

Mexican Red Sauce

About 1 cup

Or, otherwise known as salsa cruda. You will find this sauce on Mexican tables any time of day.

1 medium tomato, finely chopped
1/2 onion, chopped
1 clove garlic, minced
1 jalapeno chile, minced
1 T. chopped cilantro
1 T. lemon juice
1 tsp. vegetable oil
1/2 tsp. oregano

Mix all the ingredients together in a glass bowl. Cover and refrigerate to let flavors develop.

Salsa Fria (cold sauce)
4-6 jalapeno or serrano chilis chopped
very fine (canned green chilis
may be used)
2 large onions, chopped fine
2 " ripe tomatoes, peeled & chopped fine
3 cloves garlic
2 small bunches of cilantro, minced "   "
1/4 c red wine vinegar
1/4 c oil   (yield 2 cups)
1/4 tsp. oregano
1/2 " salt

Mix all ingred. together in a
bowl & refrigerate for at
least an hour before serving

Salsa Picante

This will add some zest to your meal. You will want to add the hot red pepper according to your taste.

1 cup tomato sauce
2 tsp. crushed dried red peppers
2 tsp. lime juice
2 tsp. cider vinegar
1/4 tsp. oregano
2 cloves garlic, minced
1 tsp. cumin

Mix all the ingredients together in a bowl.

Salsa Verde

The tomatillo version of a sauce. Serve with tortilla chips as an appetizer. It can be topped with diced avocado and cubes of a fresh white Mexican cheese.

1/2 lb. fresh tomatillos
2 serrano chiles
1/2 onion, chopped
1 T. cilantro
salt

Remove the husks from the tomatillos. Place in a saucepan, cover with water and simmer about 10 minutes or until soft. Drain.

Place in a blender with the remaining ingredients. Blend until smooth. If you overblend you will have a frothy mixture. Dilute with some water if you desire. Transfer to a serving bowl.

Variation: For an all-raw sauce, prepare with raw tomatillos, adding 1/4 cup water before blending.

Green Sauce

This is a slight variation, being an all-cooked sauce. Used in casseroles (see Chicken in Green Sauce, page 71) and is a good choice to mix with shredded chicken as a filling for tacos.

1 (14-1/2 oz) can chicken broth
1 lb. tomatillos, husked and quartered
3 serrano chiles, minced
2 garlic cloves, minced
1/2 onion, diced
1/4 cup chopped cilantro
1/2 tsp. oregano
1/4 tsp. sugar
salt and pepper, to taste

Combine all ingredients in a large saucepan. Simmer until sauce is consistency of puree, about 1 hour. Gently pierce the tomatillos with a fork as they become soft.

Optional step: Strain the sauce, return to saucepan and thicken with flour and butter or cornstarch.

Salsa Borracha

Otherwise known as "drunken sauce." A must with any grilled or barbecued meat.

1/2 cup vegetable oil
6 chiles pasilla
1 cup orange juice
salt
1 onion, finely chopped
1/4 cup tequila

In a skillet fry the chiles in the oil until they lighten in color. Drain and remove stem and seeds. Place in a blender with the orange juice and salt. Puree until smooth.

In the same oil, saute the onions until soft. Add the sauce and continue cooking for 5 minutes. Remove from heat, add the tequila and let cool.

Desserts

Mexicans have a delicious assortment of desserts which have their roots from Spain. In fact, the whole concept of desserts originated in Europe.

The greatest credit, however, should go to the Mexican nuns, whose practise was to prepare and sell their custards, puddings and candies. They also made special treats for religious holidays.

This assortment of desserts runs from the classic flan or caramel custard, to puddings and fruit, (both fresh and poached, with a sugary syrup), to their pay de gueso, which is similar to a cheesecake. Many desserts use the flavors of cinnamon, brown sugar or chocolate. There are also special sweet snacks included for the holidays.

Rice Pudding

A bit softer with a more pronounced cinnamon taste than our puddings. If you have any left over, thin with a little milk, heat and serve for breakfast.

2 cups water
1 cinnamon stick
2 strips of lime peel
1 cup uncooked long grain white rice
4 cups milk
3/4 cup sugar

1/4 tsp. salt
4 egg yolks
1/2 tsp. vanilla extract
1/2 cup raisins
1 T. butter

Bring the water to a boil in a large saucepan. Add the cinnamon and lime. Simmer 5 minutes. Add the rice and cook 25 minutes or until rice is done. Remove cinnamon and lime peel.

Simmer the milk, sugar and salt in another large saucepan 20 minutes **only** until milk takes on a slight creaminess. Add the cooked rice.

Beat yolks in a small bowl a few seconds. Stir in vanilla and 2 T. hot rice. Stir back into rice mixture along with the raisins.

Spoon into baking dish. Dot with butter. Broil 3-4 minutes until top is golden.

Flan

A baked egg custard crowned with a light caramel sauce. This is the classic Mexican dessert.

1-1/2 cups sugar
4 cups milk
1 cinnamon stick

6 eggs
pinch of salt
1 tsp. vanilla

Carmelize 1/2 cup sugar in a skillet by heating the sugar, stirring with a wood spoon, until it turns a deep brown. Pour into a 1-1/2 qt. souffle dish or flan mold, tilt the mold to coat the entire bottom and put a little up the sides of the mold.

In a large saucepan heat the milk, 1 cup sugar, cinnamon stick and salt. Let simmer 15 minutes. Let cool.

Place eggs in a bowl and beat until foamy. Add to the cooled milk along with vanilla. Remove cinnamon stick, strain, and pour into coated mold.

Set mold in a pan of hot water on lowest shelf of oven. Bake at 350° for 1-1/4 hours or until knife inserted in flan comes out clean. Let cool. Unmold on platter with some depth to hold caramel. Serve at room temperature.

There are many other ways to make the basic flan. Here are a few of them:

- Add 6 oz. finely ground almonds to the milk
- Use 1 (14 oz) can sweetened condensed milk with 2-1/4 cups regular milk
- Replace milk with 1 quart unsweetened pineapple juice
- Add 2 tsp. Kahlua and 2 tsp. dark rum
- For lighter texture, use 8 eggs
- Sprinkle 1 cup chopped pecans on top of the carmelized sugar in the mold.
- Add grated lemon or orange rind to milk
- Add 4 tsp. instant coffee to milk
- Serve in individual custard cups

Bread Pudding

Serves 8

The Mexican style pudding full of raisins, nuts and apples.

1 lb. day old French bread or Challah
water
1 tsp. cinnamon
1 cup brown sugar
3 T. vanilla extract
1 cup seedless raisins
1 cup chopped walnuts or pecans
2-1/2 cups sliced apples
butter

Tear bread into pieces and place in large mixing bowl. Moisten with enough water to make it wet but not soupy. Add remaining ingredients and mix well.
Place in a buttered 9" x 13" baking dish. Bake in 350° oven for 1 hour.

Fried Bananas

These are good any time of day. Mexicans generally view them as more of a snack than a true dessert.

4 large bananas, peeled & cut in half lengthwise
4 T. butter
1 cup brown sugar
juice of 1 orange
juice of 1 lemon
1 tsp. grated orange peel
1 tsp. grated lemon peel
Sauce:
1/2 cup sour cream
1/2 cup powdered sugar

Melt butter in large skillet and fry bananas 1 minute each side. Pour the sugar, juices and peels over the bananas. Simmer about 15 minutes. Baste with syrup while cooking. Serve with the sauce. For sauce combine sour cream and powdered sugar in small bowl.

Mango Mousse

Fresh ripe mangoes that have about the same "soft" feel as an avocado are necessary here to achieve a smooth textured mousse enriched with the flavor of almonds. Use peaches or apricots instead of mangoes. Use only 1/4 cup sugar.

4 eggs
2 egg yolks
1/2 cup sugar
2 envelopes unflavored gelatin
2 cups mashed mangoes (about 3)
3 T. brandy, Amaretto or rum
1/2 tsp. almond extract
2 cups heavy cream, whipped

In large bowl beat eggs and yolks until thick and lemon-colored. Place in saucepan with sugar and gelatin. Bring to a boil, stirring constantly. Remove from heat.

Stir in mangoes, brandy and extract. Chill until soft mounds form. Fold in whipped cream. Refrigerate until firm.

Almond Coconut Tart

Coconuts are readily available throughout Mexico. Flaked coconut and almonds make a lovely postre (or dessert).

Pastry:
1 cup flour

1 stick butter, room temperature
1/2 cup light brown sugar

Filling:
1 cup light brown sugar
2 eggs
1 T. Amaretto
1/4 tsp. salt

1-1/2 cups sweetened flaked coconut
1-1/2 cups toasted almonds,
    finely chopped
2 tsp. flour
1/2 tsp. baking powder

Pastry: In bowl cream flour, butter and sugar. Gather into a ball, wrap in plastic and refrigerate 15 minutes. Roll out dough about 1/8" thick. Press dough into 11" tart pan, trim and form edges. Refrigerate 15 minutes. Bake in 350° oven about 10 minutes or until light brown.

Filling: Whisk sugar, eggs, Amaretto and salt in bowl until blended. Stir in remaining ingredients. Pour into tart shell and bake at 350° about 20 minutes or until brown.

Let cool before serving.

Kahlua Chocolate Cheese

Even Mexicans have their version of cheesecake - pay de queso. This one is a crustless variety and is flavored with Kahlua, the coffee-flavored liqueur native to Mexico.

12 oz. cream cheese, room temperature
1/2 cup sugar
3 eggs, room temperature
7 T. whipping cream
2 T. Kahlua
3 oz. milk chocolate, coarsely chopped
Garnish:
whipped cream
shaved chocolate

In mixing bowl blend cream cheese and sugar until smooth. Beat in the eggs, one at a time. Mix in 3 T. cream and Kahlua. Pour into 8″ pie pan.

In saucepan melt the chocolate with remaining 4 T. cream. Drizzle chocolate in spiral pattern over filling. Stir with spoon to achieve marbling effect. Set in a pan with water half way up side of pie pan. Bake at 300° until firm in center, about 55 minutes. Cool completely and refrigerate overnight. Garnish with whipped cream and shaved chocolate.

Flan (page 138) ⇒

Sopaipillas

Little puffed up squares of dough, crisp and pale gold in color, sprinkled with powdered sugar and cinnamon. Dough should be rolled thin and oil should not be too hot or they won't puff up.

2 cups flour
2 tsp. baking powder
1 tsp. salt

2 T. shortening
2/3 cup lukewarm water
vegetable oil or shortening
Garnish: sugar & cinnamon or honey

Place flour, baking powder and salt in mixing bowl. Cut in shortening. Sprinkle in the water, mixing with a fork until all the flour is moistened. The dough should almost clean the side of the bowl. Form the dough into a ball, cover and refrigerate for 30 minutes.

Put 1-2" of oil in a pan. Heat to 400.°Roll the dough into a rectangle (12" x 10") on a lightly floured surface. Cut it into 2" x 3" rectangles. Fry each rectangle until puffed and golden, turning once, about 2 minutes. Lightly press them down with fork so they will bubble and puff up. Drain on paper towels. Serve at once and sprinkle with sugar and cinnamon or honey.

◀━ Fried Bananas (page 141)

Beverages

Any time of day you can find a special Mexican drink - coffee, chocolate, fruit coolers, beer, sangrias, cocktails.

Mexico and Tequila — can't have one without the other. Tequila, named for a town in Jalisco not far from Guadalajara, has the Margarita as its great fame. Tequila is distilled from the agave plant and can be white or gold (aged in oak vats). Mexcal, similar to Tequila, has the worm in the bottle which is said to give strength to anyone with the "strength" to drink it.

Mexico has many good brews of beer, served icy cold and garnished with lime and salt. Wine is just coming of age, some are quite good. The best is from Northern Baja and Querétaro. Kahula is native to Mexico as is the local and very alcoholic pulque, the distilled milky sap from the maguey or agave century plant.

Margarita

Serves 2-4

The drink that first comes to our mind when we think of Mexico. The pale-green, sweet and sour tequila drink rimmed with salt. Since there are many different formulas, here are two:

Version 1
coarse salt
3/4 cup tequila
3/4 cup triple sec
3/4 cup fresh lime juice
3/4 cup crushed ice

Version 2
coarse salt
1/2 cup tequila
1/4 cup triple sec
3/4 cup lime or lemon juice or sweet
    and sour mix

Chill 4 stemmed glasses. Run lime slice around rim and dip in coarse salt to coat. Pour tequila, triple sec, lime juice and ice into a blender. Whirl until blended. Pour into glasses.
    Simple variation: Use Rose's lime juice for the fresh lime juice, version 1, and juice of 1 lemon.

Tequila Cooler

Two drinks that combine tequila, fruit juices and grenadine.

3 cups unsweetened pineapple juice
2 cups unsweetened grapefruit juice
1 cup tequila
3 T. grenadine syrup

Combine all ingredients in a pitcher and serve over ice in tall glasses.

Tequila Sunrise

Serves 6

2-2/3 cups orange juice
1 cup tequila
1/2 cup lime juice
1/4 cup grenadine

Combine orange juice, tequila and lime juice in a pitcher. Pour over ice in glasses. **Slowly** add grenadine syrup to each glass.

Sangria

Spain gave the Mexicans their red wine punch. There are versions with lemon, lime, or orange juice. This one uses all three.

1 bottle (4/5 qt) dry red wine
1/2 cup triple sec or Cointreau
2/3 cup fresh lemon juice
1/4 cup fresh lime juice
1/4 cup fresh orange juice
Garnish:
lemon, lime and orange slices

Combine all the ingredients in a large pitcher. Chill for 30 minutes. Garnish with fruit slices.

Variation: for a "white" Sangria, try this with white wine instead of red.

Mexican Coffee

Some very good coffee is grown in Mexico and typically is brewed and sweetened with dark sugar and spices. Piloncillo is the cone-shaped unrefined Mexican sugar available in Latin American speciality stores.

6 cups water
1/4 cup piloncillo or dark brown sugar
1 cinnamon stick
3/4 cup ground coffee

Combine water, sugar and cinnamon in saucepan. Heat until sugar dissolves. Stir in coffee and simmer 2 minutes. Remove from heat and let stand 10 minutes. Strain and serve.

Optional method: Automatic drip coffee maker. Place 1/4 cup piloncillo (or dark brown sugar), 1/2 tsp. ground cinnamon and coffee in basket. Pour in 6 cups water and brew.

Variation: To 4 cups of freshly brewed coffee add 8 T. of Kahula and 6 T. of tequila. Top with whipped cream.

Mexican Hot Chocolate

A native drink of Mexico is chocolate.

6 cups milk
1/4 cup sugar
3 oz. unsweetened chocolate
1 tsp. ground cinnamon
3 eggs
2 tsp. vanilla

Garnish:
whipped cream

In saucepan, combine milk, sugar, chocolate and cinnamon. Heat until chocolate is melted. Cook and stir until mixture **almost** boils (do not boil).

In bowl, beat eggs with vanilla. Add 1 cup hot milk, then return to saucepan. Cook for 2 minutes. Beat until frothy.

Pour into mugs and garnish with whipped cream.

Hot Apple Cider

For those chilly winter afternoons and evenings.

5 cups apple juice or cider
1/4 cup fresh lemon juice
1/2 tsp. salt
1-2/3 cups tequila
1/3 cup Cointreau

Garnish:
lemon slices

Mix the apple and lemon juices in a saucepan. Bring to a simmer. Add the remaining ingredients. Heat thoroughly.
Ladle into mugs and garnish with lemon slices.

Sparkling Limeade

Lime is one of Mexico's national flavors, and this refreshing drink complements Mexican dishes.

2/3 cup sugar
1-2/3 cups fresh lime juice
5 cups sparkling mineral water

Mix the sugar and lime juice together in a pitcher. Stir well. Add water and taste. Add more sugar if necessary. Pour over ice and serve.

Index

Curry Powder

5 tbsp. hot dried red chili powder
1/2 tsp. powdered ginger
1/2 " mustard seeds
1/2 tbsp. cloves
2" stick of cinnamon
4 tbsp. coriander seed
4 tbsp cumin seeds
3 tbsp tumeric
1/2 tsp fenugreek
1/2 tsp cardamon
mix all ingredients together &
grind in a blender until fine.

METRIC CONVERSION CHART

Liquid or Dry Measuring Cup (based on an 8 ounce cup)

1/4 cup = 60 ml
1/3 cup = 80 ml
1/2 cup = 125 ml
3/4 cup = 190 ml
1 cup = 250 ml
2 cups = 500 ml

Liquid or Dry Measuring Cup (based on a 10 ounce cup)

1/4 cup = 80 ml
1/3 cup = 100 ml
1/2 cup = 150 ml
3/4 cup = 230 ml
1 cup = 300 ml
2 cups = 600 ml

Liquid or Dry Teaspoon and Tablespoon

1/4 tsp. = 1.5 ml
1/2 tsp. = 3 ml
1 tsp. = 5 ml
3 tsp. = 1 tbs. = 15 ml

Temperatures

°F		°C
200	=	100
250	=	120
275	=	140
300	=	150
325	=	160
350	=	180
375	=	190
400	=	200
425	=	220
450	=	230
475	=	240
500	=	260
550	=	280

Pan Sizes (1 inch = 25 mm)

8-inch pan (round or square) = 200 mm x 200 mm
9-inch pan (round or square) = 225 mm x 225 mm
9 x 5 x 3-inch loaf pan = 225 mm x 125 mm x 75 mm
1/4 inch thickness = 5 mm
1/8 inch thickness = 2.5 mm

Pressure Cooker

100 Kpa = 15 pounds per square inch
70 Kpa = 10 pounds per square inch
35 Kpa = 5 pounds per square inch

Mass

1 ounce = 30 g
4 ounces = 1/4 pound = 125 g
8 ounces = 1/2 pound = 250 g
16 ounces = 1 pound = 500 g
2 pounds = 1 kg

Key   (America uses an 8 ounce cup - Britain uses a 10 ounce cup)

ml = milliliter
l = liter
g = gram
K = Kilo (one thousand)
mm = millimeter
m = milli (a thousandth)
°F = degrees Fahrenheit

°C = degrees Celsius
tsp. = teaspoon
T. = tablespoon
Kpa = (pounds pressure per square inch)
    This configuration is used for pressure cookers only.

Metric equivalents are rounded to conform to existing metric measuring utensils.

Tacos (page 23) ➡
Black Beans (page 118) ➡
Refried Beans (page 120) ➡